miracle
in the
mundane

miracle
in the
mundane

//

poems, prompts, and inspiration to unlock
your creativity and unfiltered joy

//

tyler knott gregson

A TARCHERPERIGEE BOOK
NEW YORK

tarcherperigee

An imprint of Penguin Random House LLC
penguinrandomhouse.com

Most TarcherPerigee books are available at special quantity discounts for
bulk purchase for sales promotions, premiums, fund-raising, and educational
needs. Special books or book excerpts also can be created to fit specific
needs. For details, write: SpecialMarkets@penguinrandomhouse.com.

ISBN 9780525537526

Printed in the United States of America
1 3 5 7 9 10 8 6 4 2

Book design by Ashley Tucker

sly

For Sarah,
my light-chasing,
adventure-seeking,
grace-filled,
wanderlust-soaked
partner in crime.

And
to the original Chasers of the Light,
those of you who took the leap
and joined us.

contents

introduction 11

—

introduction

//

Few things spark inspiration in me like a long drive, like hours on an open road, a destination too far away to even begin getting excited for. A few years back, a long drive exactly like this threw a long road out in front of me and my fiancée, Sarah Linden. We had hours to drive, and ideas started filling the air, and before long the music was turned off to make room for our voices, for our excited and frenzied brainstorming. It was there, halfway between Montana and the middle-of-nowhere Canadian mountains, that the idea for a life-reboot course took shape. Over ten hours later, we'd come up with the foundation that would become the first-ever course we taught together, Chasers of the Light.

The ideas that Sarah and I came up with (it cannot be emphasized enough just how magical and instrumental Sarah was and continues to be in this crazy process), the challenges we cooked up on that Canadian drive, were stripped directly from the life we've always tried to lead, directly from the countless questions I've gotten from people just like you over the years. Everyone, everywhere, wants to know how to lead a more meaningful, joy-filled, connected, and creative life. Everyone, everywhere, deserves to.

If you've come this far, you are most certainly here for a reason. So, too, am I. From time to time in this crazy and chaotic spin we call life, we need to pause, reflect, and truly begin again. There is no shame in this. There is no reason for any other feeling right now than elation: elation for all the good that is coming your way, all the changes you can make to give yourself all that you deserve. Okay, maybe a little apprehension too, because you never know what crazy ideas might be in store for you. Know this: I am on your team, I've always been, and I wish for you what I wish for myself:

To live an honest, simple life, filled with creativity, joy, compassion, and a deeper, richer appreciation for the world around us.

It's a beautiful place. I just want to help you see it.

Here is what you can expect from this little book, and beyond . . .

Daily Challenges

These will be the heart of this book, and please know this is not, in fact, a writing book. This is a "life reboot" of sorts, and as such, you're going to be thrown into some challenges each day that will push you outside of your comfort zones, realign the way you might see the world, and gently guide you toward taking steps into your new life, your new way of being. This book might ask you to do some writing, but know that this is not a demand or a contest to see who can write the prettiest, the most uniquely or ornately. The writing is simply the easiest and most effective way to share with yourself, and with the other people who have found their way to this book, what you are learning, what you are struggling with, and what you might want feedback from the universe on. Sometimes, in lieu of words, you may need to take photographs, make drawings, or maybe even shoot a video, if you're brave enough to share it with the world. Sharing is, and always will be, optional, but I do encourage you to open up, to let the world in, all of us, and to accept any feedback you might receive with an open heart. A community will be built around this bravery and vulnerability, and soon you'll come to realize that there are people hiding in every corner of the planet who feel like you do, who hurt like you do, and who celebrate just like you do. We can build families in the strangest places, we can find home where we're least expecting it.

Beyond . . .

The Beyond section of some challenges is simply that—a way to go beyond, to dig deeper into the heart and message of each challenge, to push yourself a bit further outside your own carefully constructed comfort zone. This is a way to test your mettle and to learn more in the process. I urge you to try them, without worry or regard to completing every one. There is no failing this, there is no failing me or yourself. I am here to grow as you grow, to reboot my own life as you are. I cannot wait.

In Case You're Wondering

To try to address questions before they might pop up, here are a few answers to common inquiries that may find their way into your beautiful brain.

How Can I Share My Work with You?

I can promise you one thing: I will do my very best to read, and interact, as much as humanly possible, as you share your brain rain across the social media spheres. I have created a Facebook page called Miracle in the Mundane (facebook.com/miracleinthemundane) for precisely this purpose. I encourage you to join and work your way into sharing anything and everything with the others who join. We can build a community this way, a family of people scattered around the world who can give us honest feedback on our journey, as we do theirs. This book, at its heart, is a self-study, in a way, and I hope you get out of it as much as I have over the years it took to put these into practice in our own lives. The sharing, and the community that I hope is built, will be an additional instrument into finding not only yourself, but a new tribe of people who feel the same way you do. Family—home—can be found in such wonderfully strange and diverse places. I truly hope this becomes one.

Can I Miss a Day, Skip a Challenge, or Change the Rules?

The beauty of this book, of this reboot, is that there *are* no rules, and that it does not require a massive amount of time. You can do most of these challenges anywhere, at any time. Again, there are no rules, but I believe in my heart of silly hearts that you'll get more out of this experience if you do the work honestly and commit. I urge you to minimize distractions, yes even social media (until after you're done with each), while diving into your challenges. This process is for you to open up, deeply, and I want you to commit to that process and the feeling you'll get when you turn the corner on each challenge. Hopefully, you'll agree.

When Sarah and I created the course that inspired this book, and then again when I was creating the book itself, I had no idea what it would come to be. I didn't know if it was self-help, if it was a life reboot, or if it was an inspirational book aimed at spirituality and philosophy. To be frank, I still don't know precisely what this is, how to classify it, where it will end up on bookstore shelves, in your hearts, in your lives. I simply know that, over all these years of being asked the same questions from so many different people, all these years giving advice, both in person and from a distance, there are so many of you out there wishing to know how to live a life that feels bigger, that feels like it is richer, like it is *more*.

In an attempt to answer these thousands of questions, to share with all of you some of the things I've learned along my journey, I have come up with this little book and, in it, these challenges. I hope you know that these challenges might seem simple from time to time, like no-brainer advice that anyone, anywhere, could give you, but they add up to something. They add up to a fundamental shift in our way of thinking, a wind of change that we didn't see coming, and I promise you, if you go through this book and sincerely try each challenge, sincerely give yourself over to the process and embrace it without cynicism, you will change with it. I'm not going to promise you brighter colors or tastes that soar, I won't tell you that you'll find your dream job or retire at twenty-five. I'll just tell you that you'll see things differently, you'll appreciate more, you'll stop, and you'll *feel*. There is a massive world that exists right behind this one, hiding like a shadow, and I swear to you it radiates with beauty, with a simple grace altogether unexpected. There are little miracles exploding in front of our eyes every second of every day, disguised as the most mundane of things: All I want is for you to see them, as I have, as I try to every single day. Grab a spare journal, take a deep breath, and let's do this thing.

I hope you'll join me, I hope you'll begin.

These were the thoughts I dreamed,
connected, but meandering:
Life is gorgeous,
so entirely gorgeous.
Every tiny thing about it,
even the things that make our eyes wet,
even the things that feel
like they are strangling our tiny hearts.
This is one gigantic picture, and we
are all a part, we are single stitches on a
tapestry of human emotion,
we walk on a quilt of laughter
and tears and heartache and
such immense joy
and it just shines.
If you just look,
through it
all,
everything radiates.

genuine
connections

The world has shrunk smaller in a million ways, and we are closer to one another than we've ever been in human history. Only we aren't. This observation didn't require an advanced degree to bring it to light, and I am most certainly not the first to point it out, but it is saddening all the same. Technology has smoothed the wrinkles from many aspects of our lives, but it has also distanced us in a way we haven't seen before. Behind laptops and mobile phones, tablets and television screens, we have instant access to the lives and eyes of almost everyone we've ever met, even those with whom contact would have been lost years ago if not for social networking. We can, in the half blink of a moment, initiate contact with nearly anyone, even our president through his Twitter feed, but still, at what cost, and what does this type of contact actually mean?

Despite our hyper-connectedness, somewhere along the way we've lost our ability to speak with people, truly speak with them in person, with eyes finding eyes and ears ready to listen. As our fingers type faster, our thumbs more proficient, we've lost our voices in many ways. We've lost the ability to make genuine connections.

challenge //

Today, you're going to try to change all that. Even for a day. For the next twenty-four hours, make it your priority, your mission, your entire reason for being, to genuinely connect with every single person you come into contact with. Stop, breathe, and take the time to slow down and look people in the eye, to ask meaningful questions, to learn more about the people you probably come into contact with on a daily basis but have never truly connected with. Start where you are, with the baristas, the waitstaff, the cabdriver, the person who shares an elevator with you. Start with the cashier at the grocery, with your colleagues, with your own family members. Set the phone down, look away from the screen, and speak, and listen. There is an inherent shift that takes place when we do this, when we actually take the time to connect, and it's tangible. We slow, we breathe, and, what's more, we remember. The gratification we have become so accustomed to becomes less instant but much more impactful. At the close of day, when you've had time to unwind and settle in, reflect back on how different the day may have gone. Write briefly about what you learned in the process of reverting back to how we all used to converse, how it made the people you spoke with feel, how it made you feel in the process. Sometimes, it takes this reflection to understand that some temporary changes should become permanent ones. Hopefully, for you, this is one of those times.

For some of you, this may come easy. For others, this may feel like standing with your toes over the edge of a skyscraper. However you're feeling, I just encourage you to stick with this, and give yourself honestly to the process; I truly believe you'll feel it, and that feeling will last.

beyond // Taking this a step further, a bit beyond, will stretch your capacity for compassion. Think of a person you have been avoiding, for any reason at all. Think of a person who has challenged you, opposed you, or even been tough to be around, and make them your connection goal. Give yourself the freedom to open your mind up to them, what they have to say, how they see the world, and try to understand where they are coming from. It's a tough thing to "climb into [someone's] skin and walk around in it," as Atticus Finch once said, but doing so can shine a bright light onto an otherwise shadowed situation. Find that person you've been avoiding, and try to get to the root of who they are, why they behave how they behave, and you might just find yourself transformed in the process.

Repeat this mantra
over, and again,
until it sings when you're
silent,
it breathes when you
are breathless:
I can do anything
I can do anything
I can do anything
I
can do
anything.

try. try.
try. try.

We've all heard the old adage "If at first you don't succeed, try, try again." Unfortunately, that phrase leaves quite a bit out for many of us in today's day and age. What if we don't try to begin with? What if we're so afraid of failure that we convince ourselves that trying at all is a failure, and a failure we're not willing to cope with? What if we are so accustomed to thinking we cannot possibly succeed that we look to everyone, everywhere for help we don't actually need in the first place? So many of us (and I am guilty of this too) believe that in order to accomplish something, we have to find someone who is better at it than we are—someone smarter, wiser, more eloquent, funnier, stronger, whatever-er. What a tragedy, this. Asking for help is one of the most important lessons we learn as we age, knowing when we are at the limits of ourselves, be it knowledge, skill, or understanding. However, knowing when *not* to ask for help is a talent that carries just as much weight. We learn through failures, some large, some small, and they shape us into the people we become. Without these unfortunate, but vital, valleys in our lives, we can never truly reach the peaks that can follow; without learning from our own mistakes, painfully acquired along the route of attempt, we cannot learn where we went wrong, what we let slip through our fingers, how to improve. We are handcuffed by this fear of failure, stuck motionless and petrified, believing we require so much more than ourselves to be what we want, to do what we should, to try.

challenge //

Try. So often in our lives, we need gentle reminders that even the simplest challenges, the most mundane exercises, can have profound impacts on our lives. Somehow, however, we forget them. Somehow, we find ourselves locked into the ruts that we've created for ourselves, deep grooves that we cannot lift our feet from, and so we walk the same directions over the same landscapes. We forget to notice. So, simply, try. After making a brief reference list for yourself of any and all things you've been convincing yourself you're incapable of doing, go out and try. Restrict your ability to ask for help on all things that you know, deep down in that place you refuse to acknowledge, you can do for yourself. If you don't know, learn and use your apprehension as fuel to broaden your own horizons, adding skills to your life that didn't exist before. Try. Fail. Try again. Fail again. Only when you reach that aforementioned limit should you ask for help. Do this day in and day out throughout the next weeks of your life until it becomes a habit, and a habit you're not going to break. You will be shocked, and you will be proud when you come to realize that those limits you thought you had so clearly defined were not real at all. You can do all things, ALL things, if only you let yourself believe it. Please, stop believing you are incapable.

beyond // We invent a million excuses for not attempting the things we have always wished to do, finding new reasons to put off new experiences. We all have an instrument we want to play, a language we want to speak, a skill we want to develop or improve. For some reason, we don't—we wait and think we're too late to the game, too old, too busy. Take this book, this opportunity, to be the push off the starting block you needed. Begin—today. Whatever the thing is that you've convinced yourself you're incapable of starting, start. We, all of us out here, are waiting to read the book you haven't started, listen to the song you were supposed to write, hear you speak the language you'll need to go to all the places you were born to visit. This is simply an extension of the challenge we just presented you. This is a push into starting the thing you've been waiting to start, the big thing, the lingering wish in the back of your mind. So please, we urge you, try.

What haven't you seen
that you wanted to,
what life have you waited
to live?
We sit, for lifetimes we sit,
crafting excuses out of fears,
our hands bleed
from stitching them
together.
Set fire to the seams,
perfume yourself
in the smoke of your
regret.

sankalpa

Whenever you happen to be picking up this book, whether it's in the very first few days of its release, or months, years after it's been published and hopefully sold in bookstores around the world, I hope that no matter what events in your life led you to choosing this book, you understand the inherent strength, value, and beauty you have inside you. I hope that if nothing else, this book is a reminder of that strength, of that perfect resolve, even if it's been hiding, even if it's been dormant awhile. Perhaps, and I'll sit with fingers crossed as long as it takes if I must, you'll take away from this book something, anything, that makes you realize how much you already are, and how much you're always going to be. I hope you treat this book as not only a reminder, but as a wake-up call to reignite the passions and creativity your life may have been missing, to reboot yourself, to allow yourself to go forward with new passion, new joy, and new understanding of the unbelievable value you bring with you. I hope. Sometimes, we need to give that hope a hopeful push, and one of the ways to do this is with a *sankalpa*. *Sankalpa* is a Sanskrit word that means "resolve." It is a beautiful reminder that you already have within you all the tools and drive to live the life you wish, to be the person you wish to be. Simplified, it is a resolution we make going forward, an intention we give to the life we're about to live.

challenge //

Now is our chance to refill our hope, with our own *sankalpa*. Every year, a few months into the new year, many of our "I will . . ." New Year's resolutions have come and gone, forgotten and lost in the shuffle of all things. I hope, when working your way through this book and all of its challenges and prompts, that you come back to yourself, to the positivity and grace you and your life deserve. The *sankalpa* you are creating will consist of two parts, two resolves: First is your heartfelt desire, and second is your specific intention going forward. Using the present tense only, state your heartfelt desire. An extremely helpful tip on creating a *sankalpa* that is effective and rooted deeply is to focus on the way you state these. State them with confidence and strength. For example, rather than saying, "I want to be a more positive person," say, "Positivity is at the root of who I am." Always state your specific desires with actionable and definitive language. For example, rather than saying, "I will be more creative and write more," say, "Creativity is vital to help myself and others relate to the world around us, and I add to that every day." Treat these desires, these intentions, as if they are deserved things, as if they are concrete statements that do not waver. Plant this seed of a *sankalpa* and let it grow going forward. As always, you can feel free to share and post these wherever you so choose, but I urge you to also post them somewhere YOU can see them every single day. Remind yourself often that you deserve the life you are working toward. You deserve the joy.

beyond// *Daunting* is a word that comes to mind when it comes to creating resolutions, resolves, or heartfelt desires that should span months, that should bridge a year. Looking forward is much more challenging than looking back. It's why nostalgia has such a fierce pull on us, why we crave songs, movies, or even seasons that remind us of simpler times, of being simpler people. I know this, I understand. To go beyond here, I'm going to actually ask you to do exactly that, simplify and aim a bit lower, just a little more often. After creating your *sankalpa*, I want you to then take away some of the overwhelmed feelings that can arise after creating an intention for the year to come and, instead, make it an actionable weekly habit that breaks down some of your much larger intentions into smaller, more manageable ones. Starting now, create "mini *sankalpa*" that span no longer than the week ahead, no further than the weekend you may be craving, the adventure somewhere along the way. Create heartfelt desires for the person you wish to be over the next seven days, the kindness you wish to give, the joy you have earned, the passion you're building upon. Repeat this weekly before beginning your trek back into each new beginning, and post it somewhere you can see before leaving each day, before wandering back into the life you've built.

Will we collect them, one by one,
the remains of the ink on our fingerprints,
on the opposite pages, reminders
in reverse, of where we've wandered?
Will we hit the mark, the grand total
of protected places, the sacred bits
of sunlight, of sea? There is time, but
not much, and we must fill it with
wonder, with adventure seeping
in all the cracks the waiting caused,
those will be the doorways
for joy to enter, those will be
the windows for the breezes
carried from everywhere,
but here.

new reasons
to gather

Human beings are inherently social creatures. We like to gather, group, and share in memories and experiences, and we find a lot of unique ways to do so. As times have changed, technological advances have exploded into view, and new forms of communication were created, and we've gotten less social in many ways, isolated though connected, digitally tethered but adrift. Still, we gather for a lot of the same reasons, and as we get older, they all tend to be centered around food and drink, and entertainment ranging from brewfests to concerts, movies to plays, house parties to clubs. While all of these are amazing ways to connect, to combine with other like-minded and inspired people, they aren't the only options. And sometimes, a subtle shift in how we gather can go a long way toward not only our inspiration, but also our happiness. What if we combined our social needs with things that leave us completely breathless? What if we shared memories that were centered not on food and drink, but on discovery, on awe? What if we opened our eyes just a bit wider and saw so much more together?

challenge //

Think outside the box. Yes, even further than that, outside the room, the building, the neighborhood, the city you may find yourself in. What if we let Mother Nature be our party planner, and instead of breweries and concerts, we schedule our social events around meteor showers or full moons? What if we plan parties around bird migrations, scenic photographic hikes, or camping trips? For this challenge, do what you already do best: Gather. Only this time, instead of the tried-and-true methods we're all so used to, plan and execute a get-together with a few people, as many as you wish, that's not centered around the crutches we're so accustomed to. Throw Mother Nature into the mix and do something centered around exploration, discovery, wonder, and awe. You do not have to go far; you do not have to hop on a plane or wander off into the wild unknown. Go where you can, even if it's a walk through the most scenic places in your own urban environment. Stepping outside the box will open the door for so many different forms of inspiration to sink in, and sharing those memories will spread that through to others. Make this a habit, and you'll see the same positive effects trickle down into so many different aspects of your life.

beyond // I wonder, what would happen if this challenge happened every single month, like clockwork? Think of it as Adult Girl Scouts, and we can bring all the cookies we want. For this beyond challenge, I thought it would be absolutely magical to create a new club of explorers that gather once a month to do something exactly like this. There are calendars through the Nature Conservancy that are geographically based, and there are apps that are designed specifically to chart and plan for various different natural phenomena, everything from meteor showers to aurora borealis sightings to massive concentrations of fireflies in different forests. Using these as your guide, create a club of sorts that meets and gathers monthly to celebrate the vast and amazing planet we call home. Start small, even two members will do, and build from there. The inspiration that will come will shift the foundations of us, the trajectories of our perceptions, I promise, and you'll find yourself looking forward to it in a way you didn't see coming. Here's to the Adult Girl Scouts and all the cookies we will bring along.

Two things at once, often more.
Fierce, but tender,
    calm, but a volcano
    of worry and nerve;
    strength unmatched,
      with softness perched
        atop.
                You,
        you of poles,
    of wild opposites

        discovering
        harmony.

juxtapositions

All around us, often hiding in plain sight, are jaw-droppingly beautiful examples of two startling opposites coexisting harmoniously, side by side. We're presented with so many different instances of this, and the vast majority of them go completely unnoticed, completely unappreciated. Life beside death, construction sharing a space with destruction, calm inside of so much noise. The more mindful we become in our lives, the more trends we should see emerging, the more common threads that, in a sense, weave not only this book, but the rest of our lives together, and one of these threads is the art of observation, the art of noticing. We become accustomed to looking for patterns, noticing repetition in so many of our different senses, be it rows of buildings that all look the same, or the same sounds filling our ears at regular intervals. What can be much more of a challenge is finding opposites sharing a space, finding literal and symbolic antonyms cohabitating somewhere in our own daily lives. When we open our eyes and begin transforming how we see the world we live in, allowing in more detail in every possible way, we see more, we recognize more, and, in turn, we're inspired by, yes, you guessed it, more. My hope throughout this book, and throughout your life, is that the challenges you undergo help bring about transformation, that they act like an alarm clock to your sleepy soul, pulling you out of whatever hazes you may have found yourself in, and present to you a world brand new, a world that has always been there, hiding in all these juxtapositions we only have to seek out.

challenge //

We're going opposite hunting, and you can bring with you a camera, or a notebook, or even your favorite digital device to capture what you find. You're going on a scavenger hunt looking for juxtapositions that live all around you. Find anything from beautiful flowers growing out of junk piles or broken concrete, find life with death, find the old snuggled up to the new, find bright with dark, find young with old. Find them all, and in doing so, strengthen those muscles of observation. The more we practice *seeing* the world, truly seeing it for all it holds, all those little miracles in the mundane, the easier it becomes to find it again. The easier it becomes, the more natural it feels, the more it simply becomes how we always see. This is the point of why we're here, this is what we're made for: soaking up as much beauty as humanly possible, and showing your interpretation of it for everyone else to soak up and enjoy, and so on, and so on, forever.

beyond // One of the most fascinating and important elements of human beings is our capacity to hold within us juxtaposing traits, viewpoints, and quirks. We bipedal, furless mammals have an innate and seemingly infinite potentiality for oxymora living happily inside us, beaming out with each beat of our fragile little hearts. Finding these in people we converse with is always exciting, sometimes frustrating, and mostly humorous, and it's why I would like you to look for them. Some of the most interesting people I've ever known are walking juxtapositions, living, breathing oxymora that always keep you on your toes. Seek out these in the people you know; find two or more opposing traits that seem to live in harmony in one person. Write of these, tell of these, or, if one's juxtapositions happen to be visual, by all means photograph them. I love these quirky souls. When you're finished, it's time to throw those powers of observation onto yourself; it's time to find those juxtapositions in you. Look for these, highlight the ways you're filled with opposites, explain to yourself, to the world, how these all seem to work, how they all come together to form the finished picture of who you are.

Through the streets
we're drug
by all we refuse
to let go of.
We tether ourselves
to the horses
of regret,
and cannot understand
the dust on our
clothes.

regret vs. pride

Life is confusing, the way we hold on so tightly to some things but resist others so fiercely. One area I have seen this in myself and in the lives of those I love and spend time with is regret and pride. I have seen so many suffer so much from regret, from things left unsaid, undone, unchecked, or unresolved. I, too, have done the same. We carry these burdens of regret for things we cannot change, we mourn decisions made when we were different people, in different places, believing different things. Regrets flow into us with such ease, and we refuse to let them go, torturing ourselves incessantly and unnecessarily. With pride, however, with self-confidence and self-esteem, we're quite the opposite. We are hard on ourselves and refuse with a stonewall resolve to acknowledge the good we've done, the good we are. We see light in others and offer praise for what we find, but in ourselves, we see nothing but the shadows. Why we do this, why we hold ourselves to the flame for things we wish we could have done differently but do not raise that flame above our heads in victory for the things that, deep down, we know we've done right, remains a mystery. Whatever the reason, whatever the cause for this discrepancy, it's something we need to undo. If we cannot appreciate ourselves for the successes in our lives, how can we ever begin to heal from the failures?

challenge //

Introspection is the name of this game, and no one ever said taking long, lingering looks into what makes you tick is easy. The idea here is that we're going to unearth some often startling differences in how we process our own self-images, how we see ourselves on a daily basis maybe without even realizing it. Here's what I would like you to do: Make a list with two columns. In the left column, write five to ten regrets. These can be anything you regret, from the large life-changing thing to not calling your mother back yesterday, it doesn't matter. Obviously I always prefer you dig deeper, look further inside, and try to uncover hidden truths, but sometimes it takes small steps to reach faraway destinations. Start here. In the other column, on the right, write five to ten things you're proud of accomplishing. Once again, these can be anything, of any size, but find out what it is that truly makes you feel pride for where you find yourself these days. Find them. Once you've completed your lists, step back and take note of the similarities in all your regrets and all the differences in your accomplishments. If you're anything like me, the regrets list will seem to have a common thread that glues it together, a focus, even if you didn't intend on it. For some reason, my accomplishments list seemed much harder to finish, with variations I didn't see coming. If you found something similar to what I found, write about why we are more diverse in our pride than we are in our shame. If not, write about the opposite. Dive into your regrets, into your pride, and find out more about yourself.

beyond // As we all know, regrets are invaluable teachers. Few things can help steer the future direction of our ships more than learning from the wrong turns along the way. To dig deeper into this exercise, and into yourself, write what you learned from each regret. What mistakes will you never make again? Sometimes we must illuminate the shadows we would rather keep in the dark in order to truly learn from them. Trust me, this is not as scary as it may sound.

We can hurt them
or heal,
hold on or holler
them away.
We are defined
by the choices we make,
the warm glow
of compassion,
when none is returned.
We become
the love we decide
to give.

a gentle
reconnection

People are drifting creatures. We exist on a strange sea of soil, and it's always moving, whether we feel it or not. Like continents, over the course of our lives we end up hundreds of miles from where we began, tiny pieces of ourselves break off and float away, and only from a distance can we see how they once fit. People are drifting creatures, and eventually, the vast majority of them will drift out of our lives. We can still see where they once fit, but we leave them there, and we blame the ocean of water between us. The longer we spend on this planet, the more people we drift away from. We look back at photos of us in our youth and see the single continent we once made, this strange Pangaea that we called home. We know how far we've come now, we recognize the gaps, the seas that divide our friendships, our families, our lives, but most often we don't know how it occurred. What we forget, in this isolation, is that we are not alone, and we do not have to stay here, we do not have to remain shipwrecked from those we care for, those we love, those we miss.

challenge //

Sail the stormy seas back to one of those lost islands, brave the swells, and reconnect. Find someone whose loss you feel most prominently, someone you have wanted to find again but have been hesitant to, and make contact. This will not be easy, but it will be worth it. Be patient and give them the chance to see you on their terms, to choose the way, the place, the time, and meet them how they wish. When you do, listen. Just listen. Let them pour it out, let them open up, let them speak of the way life on their island has shifted since you drifted apart. Listen, hear, and understand.

beyond // As I will ask you to do often in this book, please reflect. It may seem unnecessary, but it's this reflection, and it's the act of writing it down, that causes us to absorb what we've learned and discovered on a deeper level. After you complete this gentle re-connection, write, for yourself or for others, what you learned in your conversation with the person you sailed back to. Did anything lead to the drift? Was there anything that could have been done to prevent it, or was it a natural thing, an evolutionary separation that was blameless and organic? Is this a person you want to continue to reconnect with? Why? Ask yourself as many or as few questions as you wish, but allow yourself to expound on what happened, what should happen going forward, and how you've both changed. Sometimes it takes the mirror of someone else to recognize shifts in ourselves, both positive and nega-tive. Go beyond, and see what you find.

The poetry isn't the words,
it's not the punctuation
or the line gaps,
not the rhyme
or the typewriter that forms
the letters.
The poetry is the aching,
the empty pit
that I cannot seem to fill,
the breath I lost
and could never catch
again.

take an ache,
make it sing

Without poetry, I would not be here. Without poetry, I would not be speaking to you all in this book, meeting so many of you at book signings and events around the world. Without poetry, I do not know where I would have ended up, but it most certainly would not have been here. Without the aching, I would not have poetry. Without the aching, I would never have found the words, never have known to give them a voice, never have known to let them sing. As the poem that begins this section mentions, I was asked once what poetry was to me, and that was the only answer I knew to give it. It's taking that ache, and making it sing. It does not matter what the song sounds like, it does not matter what the lyrics end up being, it's just giving all the aches in you, the positive and the negative, the space to realize themselves. It's giving yourself room to feel them, all of them, as high and as low as they may take you.

challenge // Now, right now, is your chance to take your aches, and make them sing. We all have aches, more than we sometimes feel we can carry, and now we must give them a voice, give them a melody and a sound all their own. This one may feel awkward for you, it may feel foreign, and that is perfectly okay. Try your hand at poetry, long form or short, haiku or sonnet or free verse, it doesn't matter. Write a poem, even if it's your first, about something or someone you are passionate about, that you are aching for or from. Try your very hardest not to edit. Let your emotions be the guide, and let the poem that is created serve as a brief snapshot of exactly how you feel, exactly who you are, right now. Write for yourself, honestly and openly, and let the words fall out how they wish. As always, sharing this is optional, but I know without a shadow of a doubt we would all love to read.

beyond // It's a universal truth that we all hate the sound of our own voice. Speaking for myself, I detest hearing my own recorded voice played back. This beyond is to jump right into that self-conscious feeling and to record yourself reading your poem aloud. However you want to do it, record the spoken-word version of the poem you have just written, putting all the inflections where you, the author, intended on them residing. Read it, record it, and let others know how it was meant to be heard. You can share it or not, but allow yourself to *hear* it for the very first time.

It doesn't matter if a damn person
cares, it doesn't matter
if a single set of eyes
finds these words.
I wrote them,
I was here, once,
and for years I poured it all out.

I've never seen a puddle
pay any mind
to whether or not
it is splashed in.
Rainstorms don't bother
with who is dancing
beneath them.

an audience
of one

What is it that draws us to the art we love? What is it that captures us, sucks us in, and makes us believe so deeply in it? If you are at all like me, it's honesty. It's real, un-fakeable, vulnerable truth. Nothing takes you out of interacting with art more than the feeling that you are not looking at, listening to, or witnessing actual, honest art; nothing removes us more than feeling like we're simply looking at what the artist thought we wanted to see, pandering to some ideal we didn't have a say in. When we create art without fear, worry, or even concern for the viewer, for the recipient, something changes in us and in the creations we end up with. *We* come through. Beyond this most obvious drawback to creating unoriginal works, pieces we don't believe in, stand behind, or shine through, is another, and that is sustainability. I have always believed it may be possible to fake it for a while, whatever *it* may be, but eventually, if it's not honest, it's not going to last. For me, there is nothing more beautiful than honest art that speaks to the condition of the artist, that shines a light for a moment, however brief, however dim, onto the truth of their soul. I believe there is nothing more beautiful than when an artist creates because they simply cannot *not*, when it's an imperative that keeps them alive, when it keeps them in a state of constant wonder. This is what we should aim for.

challenge //

This challenge may be slightly terrifying, it may be something you've put off doing for, well, maybe forever, but I'm going to ask you to do it anyway. I know we all have little pieces of our creativity that we're simply afraid to share, that we don't want other people reading, seeing, or hearing, because we don't know if they'll like it, we don't know if it will be enjoyed or ridiculed. What if we took those creations, those honest and truth-filled bits that we wrote for ourselves only, and started there? What if we shared those pieces, and didn't worry about the response? What if we realized that here, at this place, is our actual and honest voice? I want you to share, with whomever you choose, your most intimate and *real* creations. Let others soak them in, let them receive them without worry of how they'll receive them. Share openly, honestly, and make this your foundation going forward. We live in an increasingly manufactured society. Everything feels fake, strained, forced, and patronizing. We can begin again, with authenticity and originality that belongs to us, and only us. And so we shall.

beyond // Now is the time to flip this challenge completely on its head. That's right, I want you to basically go against every single thing I said in the challenge. Go make art that is NOT you at all. Actively try to create something that is just for others, pandering to them only. Take yourself out of the equation and come up with something that in no way represents you but represents what you think people want from you. Give yourself over to every critique, every request, everything that you have always worked so hard to avoid. Once complete, take a moment to contrast this feeling to how you felt when completing the original challenge above, when legitimately working for yourself only. I hope the difference is staggering, I hope you are inspired by how much more enjoyment comes from creating art for yourself rather than for the perceived demands of others.

I think people
so often
forget
that the word
alone
does not
and never has
lived inside
the word
lonely.

alone vs. lonely

Who are we when reduced down, when all noise and distraction are stripped away? Who are we in the quiet moments, the bits without dialogue, without someone to remind us? This is an avoidable question, and one we often do not ask. We find ourselves trapped in the misconception that for a thing to be meaningful, it must be shared, and so we wait. We wait and we put off the things we wish to do, believing that it's only worth doing if it's done with someone else; we believe this because we are dependent, and we are dependent because it can be scary, it can be lonely, and it can be hard to do things on your own. Let's face it: We're conditioned by a million sources to believe that the only way through this life is with constant companionship. Somewhere along the way, amidst this bombardment of reminders from every other person who has a partner to share things with, we feel that if we do not also have someone to share things with, we cannot experience anything, we cannot do, really, anything at all. This is wrong. Painfully so.

challenge //

Make a list, however many entries long, of all the things you've really wanted to do, see, or accomplish over the last few years. This list can be sprawling, or it can be a single entry. It all depends on you and your passions. Make this list and review it, and beside it, make another list of all the reasons you thought you had to do it with someone else. Finally, make a third list, beside this one, of all the reasons why you could, and should, do it alone. Once all your lists are complete, choose an item off your list, either at random or with intent, and decide to do it. This will not be easy; it will most likely be terrifying, and you may want to come up with three thousand reasons why you should just wait, again, and put it off for another day. Choose your adventure, and, if for the very first time, force yourself to do it.

I'm not going to lie to you and say that some things in life are not better shared. I won't patronize you and say that anything, everything, can be done this way. I know the value of a shared life, I know how some memories are better when divided over two, or over many, who matter. I know this. What I also know is that we trick ourselves into believing that everything must be done this way, and that if we cannot share it, we cannot experience it. As I mentioned, this is wrong. Painfully so. We find ourselves when we're alone, when it's all stripped down and we stare down an experience, a memory, a transformative moment with only ourselves as witness; we find ourselves when we, feeling lonely when alone, step forward anyway and find joy.

beyond// As I mentioned, there are plenty of things that are best done in groups or, at the very least, with someone else. I know this to be true, and loneliness can sometimes come when those events or occasions arise and we've no one to accompany us. What if we could take it back? What if we could find beauty in being alone even in activities that are traditionally done with two or more people? What if we tried? For this beyond, choose any activity or situation that is almost always done with at least one other person, and do it alone. Go to dinner at a nice restaurant all by yourself, attend a concert with no one on your arm, dance in a club without anyone walking in with you, have a picnic in a park, or—and this is my favorite—take a road trip alone to somewhere you've always wanted to see. Roll the windows down, choose your favorite music the entire journey, and sing at the top of your lungs. There is freedom in the solitary, there is beauty . . . Just look.

Grant us eyes of piercing strength,
let us see beneath the skin,
around the bones, below
the blood that flows. Gift us
with this ability, for we are not
this body, not this decoration,
not this fragile frame that began
as starlight, and will end as ash.
We have always been different,
more beautiful for it, a million shades
of paint on a single canvas, spinning
in the silence; who are we to assign value
to a hue, who are we
to make such decisions? Does
the sea care whose skin it covers,
does the air choose certain lungs
to fill?

Grant us eyes of piercing strength,
eyes that see a billion colors
and find them all
beautiful.

it's bigger than you

There are elements of every religion, every spirituality, that the world could benefit from adopting. There are pieces of every different belief system that, quite simply, got it right. There is one belief system, however, that I believe everyone, everywhere should adopt if we want this world to end up in a better place than it currently finds itself. Meditation and, most specifically, meditation on compassion. I have no doubt that, for reasons that could be debated and argued over for centuries, our society has leaned into a new sphere of self-centeredness and self-obsession. We can blame the internet, smartphones, that damn rap music or violent video games or whatever other convenient and altogether probably wrong scapegoat you choose, but the fact remains: We are a culture dominated by the self, and it's getting worse in many ways. Mistake this not, I say this not in a hopeless tone, not in a sorrowful voice that cracks and vanishes into the air around us, but in a voice wrapped up in a fierce determination. I say it in protest, in defiance of the trend that we are all victims of. This does not have to remain, this does not have to stand. We have all we need to make this change, we have all the tools for this rebellion, and one of the most important in our arsenal is meditation.

challenge //

If you've never meditated before and this book is your first introduction to it, I could not be more excited for you to begin, for you to reap the benefits meditation inherently brings with it, for it to change your life, too. For this challenge, I simply want you to sit in a quiet place, close your eyes, and, for the first few minutes, focus on nothing but the breath you're bringing into your body and the breath you're letting gently go. When you feel settled, centered, I simply want you to meditate on the thought of others, beginning with those closest to you. Allow thoughts to enter and exit as they wish, acknowledging them as they come and go, but try to softly steer them toward the suffering of those you know and love. Feel the pains they may be experiencing. Feel their joys as well, but feel them. Meditate further, including people who may not be as close but who you know, be they acquaintances, friends of friends, distant family members, and the like. Feel compassion for their trials, tribulations, and experiences. Let the weight of them sink into you while you sit quietly. Finally, meditate deeper by including strangers, people you have, only by proxy or happenstance, come into contact with. These can be people from news reports, people you pass on the road, people standing near you in line at the grocery store, it doesn't matter. Even if you must imagine and invent the happenings in their life, allow your mind to wander and see their innocence, their vulnerability, their much-needed peace. Going back to your breath, inhale deeply the sadness and suffering of all others, absorbing it into your lungs, and exhale calm and joy. Each breath refilling the voids that such suffering can leave, with peace. For this challenge, this is all I wish you to do: Remove your mind from the sometimes seemingly infinite back onto yourself, to understand that everyone, everywhere, is deserving of compassion, and most specifically, you.

beyond // There are two ways I wish for you to take this challenge further. Both will stretch you, both are vital. First, do this entire exercise again, and this time after the last step of compassionate incorporation, add a final layer of people to your thoughts: people who you do not, in any way, feel they deserve it. Find the people who, in your mind, have hurt you, hurt others, done wrong, and have treated you in any way that you feel is unworthy of your compassion. Find the "enemies," real or imagined. The Dalai Lama, one of the most inspirational and wonderful human beings to ever grace this planet with his presence, often teaches that our enemies are our greatest teachers, for no one else can truly test our patience and capacity for compassion. Begin here. Meditate on their actions and seek out the reasons behind them, seek out the pain that led to the anger that's hiding beneath the anger itself. Meditate deeply on the sadnesses and aches that could lead to behavior that repelled you, and others, from them. This will hurt, this will be extremely difficult, and this is so very important. Try.

Finally, to take this even further, I just ask for your time. Do this exercise daily, every single day, even if it's only for ten minutes right before you step out of bed or right before you step back into it. I cannot tell you how worth it this truly is.

Will I be an old man, singing to the seals
as they pass by the sound, will I holler into the loch
and wait for the sound of my own voice
to return, only older, only slower.
Maybe this is a road that's always been
heading there, a destination before I knew
of the journey that would unfold. Maybe
I have been practicing those songs,
all my life.

I can see it, the rain shadow and the squall,
there is sea foam on the sand.
There is a sadness to this.

Look for the crazy old wanderer, hair
wind tossed and careless, look for the
weather worn smile, the eyes wrinkle
carved. This road has been winding,
but heading East.
There is salt in the wind.

human sampling

No, I'm not asking you for your DNA. I'm not going to research your ancestry. I'm not going to clone you, even though I've no doubt you're worthy of that honor. What I'm after are stories, and there are stories everywhere, absolutely everywhere. Each person, each beautiful stranger we walk by on the street, sit next to on the train, stand in line with at coffee shops, or eat beside in restaurants, each has their own stories, and they are the star of them. We forget this somewhere along the way, forget that in the novel of our lives, we're surrounded by characters who have a novel of their own unfolding in front of our eyes. By giving these characters the time and respect they deserve, it opens up our capacity for understanding and, in the process, transforms the way we see our own story. What is wonderful is that in our lives we are presented with hundreds and hundreds of opportunities to practice this mindful way of seeing the people who float in and out. We are given a thousand chances to chronicle these fleeting strangers, to use them as an exercise to more fully develop their characters in our own story.

challenge // The trick is finding the deeper story in all of us or, at the very least, inventing it. For this challenge, go to your favorite public place, be it a coffee shop, restaurant, library, wherever, and begin truly seeing people. With a notebook, or your favorite digital device if it is easier, write fully formed descriptions of five people you find interesting, for whatever reason. Describe them entirely and deeper than surface level, as if they are real characters in a real novel or film. What's more, find the reasons behind the details you notice, see the humanity behind it all. Characters and the development of them are such an integral part of storytelling. This is your chance to develop that skill for not only your creativity, but for your own compassionate viewpoint as well. We all have stories, we just have to find them.

beyond // Speculation in this case is an amazing catalyst for creativity, but it's still speculation. We are still guessing, inventing histories and motivations, inventing the "why" behind the "what." We still don't know. Now is our chance to find out. If, and only if, you feel safe, start a conversation with any one of the people you've described. Look into their eyes. Hear their story. Find out all the ways you were right, but, mostly, all the ways you were wrong. Once you've finished, apply this new knowledge to a new description, write them again, more deeply, and discover just how far actual understanding can go.

Balanced between worlds,
I sway back
and forth. How often
the voices call me home,
how often
I want to give in to
the nostalgia,
lose my mind chasing the way
Autumn's first chill
makes me travel
in time.
I am held here by
rusted metal
below the surface
of my seas.
I look up to the trees,
the mountain that
holds them,
to the fog,
and I am called.
I am pulled.

How light this anchor
feels,
how strong the
current.

a change
is gonna come

I know, we've all heard that it is impossible to step into the same river twice. As we grow, continuing down this strange path, we begin to realize that we'll never even see the same river twice, let alone get close enough to put our feet back into it. Change is an absolute and unconquerable reality, and yet we fight tooth and nail all our lives trying to resist it, trying to convince ourselves that it doesn't really exist. Inevitably, we fail, and fail, and fail again, but still, we try. Such sorrow rises when this occurs, such smothering nostalgia, and not only does it paint our days in anxiety and apprehension, but it stains the future as well. So much of our lives become lost in the pursuit of stasis, we strain and waste so much joy hoping that all things will remain the same. In this ineffective striving, we forget something that time and experience have taught us numerous times throughout our lives. We forget that sometimes change is precisely what we need. Without change, doors to new experiences, new people, new happiness would never be opened. When we forget this, we paint things the way they once were, mistakenly believing it is the way they should ever be. Quite simply, we forget that change, despite being an inevitability we'll always have to deal with, is also the instrument of some of the biggest positive shifts in our entire lives.

challenge // Dealing with change, accepting it, is in and of itself a challenge we face constantly over the span of our lives. We can never outrun it, we can never wish it away. I know this and, as such, I recognize and appreciate the seemingly insurmountable task of accepting that fact. What we're going to do in this challenge is hopefully help make that a bit easier. What I wish you to do is to simply make a list, as long or as short as you would like, of transitions in your life or moments when you had to make a decision over the last five to ten years. These should be moments when you felt fearful, apprehensive, timid, or reluctant to have change in your life. Put as much detail as you can, for the more you write of it, the deeper you go into the memory of how you felt before the changes took place, the more full a picture you'll have of your emotional state. Write about who you were behind the fears that you held, what you were doing, how you thought the change would directly impact everything that surrounded you. First, write all the fears, all the things you didn't want to change and held on to so tightly, write about them all and the consequences you swore were on the horizon if that change should take place. Changing jobs? Moving? Ending a relationship? Whatever the case, whatever the change may have been, write of why you were so reluctant to have it actually transpire. Read these over once you've completed your list, soak them all in and absorb the way you felt at that time, however distant, however fresh. Now, start a new list as a direct companion to the first. For each entry, write how the change actually did impact your life, beyond the imagined results you first wrote of. Write about any positive outcomes that came only because the changes took place. Find them all, each and every door that was opened because of it, each slice of joy, each unexpected grace that added up to bring you back to where you are today. Even if you must dig deep, highlight every possible positive result, and once you've done this, write about how you did, in fact, survive the negative ones. Write about how you *were* able to overcome the things you swore you could not. Be proud of the way you survived the changes you felt would be dire, be proud of the way you survive.

beyond // To take this a step further, we're going to begin the cycle again, and allow yourself to project into the future. This time, however, you hopefully see things with new eyes, with new optimism. Write a new list of five to ten things you're currently afraid or anxious about changing in your life. Write about what the changes would do to you, what they could mean for the happiness in your life. Write about the way you feel about these potential consequences, however remote the chance of them actually occurring. Once you've finished, underneath each entry, using the same mentality and clarity from this challenge, write about possible positive outcomes that may come about if each change were to take place. Write about how you could survive it and perhaps even thrive from it. Restructuring the way we see change is a vital component of living a mindful and joy-filled life. Start now.

I say it but it is not believed,
I have never, not once,
felt pride
for anything I have achieved,
made, created, or shared.
Never, do I feel pride for who I am,
or who I have become,
or who I may one day evolve into.
I lack this emotion, I feel it not,
any time or circumstance in my life,
save One:
When I, simple handed and tender souled,
reach across that breathless emptiness
between my own fingers and a wild thing,
and am allowed, by their grace and
trust and understanding, to touch.
It is here, only, that I am proud of the heart
that beats in my chest, of the gentleness
that was never scared away from me;
The soul in me that tells them, wild and
unruled and perfect them: I am here,
and I will never hurt you.
You are safe
with me.

disney princess

I've been called a lot of things in my life, some good, some bad. Some bad things disguised as good things, some good things that, when I thought deeper about them, turned out to be bad things. Of all, the one that to this very day I still love the most is when I was called a Disney princess. I was given this title because I love living things—all living things of all shapes, sizes, species, and types. I love finding them, especially the wild ones, connecting with them, holding them in my hands, speaking to them, and for a brief moment bridging the gap between us. There is an extremely important lesson in this, in the desire to show all sentient beings that not only do you care about their well-being and happiness, but you love them and want to connect, want to feel their life force for a time. To me, this extends beyond Buddhism, beyond spirituality, beyond everything else, and simply highlights how every single living creature deserves our love, respect, and care. When we begin living this way, when we begin to go beyond just noticing all the life that pulses around us, it changes us, it connects us and grounds us in a way I don't think any of you will see coming.

challenge // For the next twenty-four to forty-eight hours, become your very own Disney princess. I'm not going to ask you to go out of your way to hold any animals, any creepy-crawly insects, or any rodents that could be carrying diseases you don't even want to imagine, but I will ask you to do this: Start paying attention to every living creature that is existing in its own life, all around you. Begin by finding them, noticing them, stopping to give them the attention they deserve. After you feel more comfortable with finding and noticing, try reaching out. Take the time to stop and pet the dogs that walk by you, take the time to pick up the beetles that are at risk from being crushed on the sidewalks, let the ladybugs explore your fingertips, stand quiet and calm as squirrels explore around you, as birds land. We get so busy living our own lives, we forget we're just one of trillions of lives being lived concurrently. We forget that everything has a place, every life has a role, a beautiful purpose, not just us. When you get back home from your days of Disney princess wandering, write about the different life-forms you found, write about your connection with them, your interaction, however brief. Feel free to photograph the creatures you spend time with; make it easier to remind yourself in the days, weeks, and months to come. This is a repeatable challenge, this is a life change that will stick with you.

beyond // Cuddling, petting, loving, and appreciating a new puppy, an adorable kitten, or a fluffy creature you stumble upon is easy, it comes naturally to us. What's more difficult is finding something to appreciate in creatures that normally bring with them negative connotations. What about spiders? What of beetles, cockroaches, bees, or grasshoppers? Can we love them too? We can, and we should. The true test of our capacity for kindness and compassion when it comes to other living things, the true test of our innate Disney princess-ness, is if we're able to extend these kindnesses to creatures that normally repel us. To take this challenge into the beyond stage, I simply want you to try. For the next thirty days, instead of killing the little creatures that find their way into your life, your apartment, your house, give them the love and respect they deserve. Move them to new homes outside if you cannot abide them in your home, carry them gently to somewhere they can live out their own life. When outside, take the time to notice the ants, the bees, the beetles, or spiders. Find intricacies that are worthy of appreciation, understand that they have a life completely separate from your own, and it deserves the exact same amount of love and respect that yours does. I have not taken the life of any living creature knowingly in the last twenty-five years of my life, and it may seem small, but it creates a fundamental shift into knowing our own place in the cosmos, by shrinking our focus down into things that have always been at our mercy.

We can forgive those
who forgot us,
we can set down the burden
and walk away
untethered.
Why do we carry
the corpses of cruelty,
the dead weight
of betrayal?

a compassionate mind

Would it be a stretch to say that of all things, right now we need reasons to unite us, the collective us, as we stand divided and split? Would it be a stretch to say that there are forces at work that only further push us apart, that drive wedges between us and turn the cranks to keep the pressure in the middle, right on the fragile and tender fracture points? Unfortunately, I believe, it's not a stretch, it's the reality we're presented with on a daily basis. We are tested every hour of the day and night, our compassion and capacity for understanding pushed to the limits. If we're not careful, we can become predisposed to carrying weight that we've got no business carrying. We hold on to anger, irritation, frustration, and blame, and we forget about the negative consequences inflicted upon us when doing so. Without directly noticing, it shifts our perspective, it paints everything in colors we didn't intend, and it reframes the way we see every single thing. Before we know it, even the good bits lose their luster, even the positive moments seem tainted. These broad divides leak their way locally, into our own homes, our own hearts. We begin to feel divided from those we should feel connected to. This tragedy should not be allowed to stand, it should not be allowed to stay. We are built for more, and we sell ourselves and our lives short when we do not actively fight to change this. We need more compassion, not less. We need more forgiveness, not more blame. As most important things, it is so much easier to say than to do, to practice rather than to preach, but I hope you find it worth it to begin practicing, to begin doing. What better time than now? What better a place than right in front of our own eyes?

challenge// This challenge—developing a compassionate mind—is one that will stay with you for the rest of your life, and will continue to stimulate you throughout it. In all honesty, sustaining compassion is insanely difficult. We are tested daily from nearly every angle. Until we realize that we are in control of our compassion, our forgiveness, our understanding, we will be slaves to reactionary forces within ourselves. Forgiveness is a skill that requires great practice, at what can often feel like great personal sacrifice. Reframing this and how we view forgiveness can be an integral part of unlocking not only our own compassionate minds, but also a new depth of positivity and calm toward the entire world around us. To gently help yourself along this path, write a letter or two to people in your life who you've been carrying any form of anger, irritation, or ill will toward, and offer your heartfelt forgiveness for whatever part they may have played. Carry no grudges, and let the past truly become a past. We know the weight of the anger we carry, we feel it every day, so why wouldn't we set it down? Why not relieve ourselves of that burden and, in the process, the burdens of those who wish our forgiveness? Why not, indeed? Once you've completed this, start over. Only this time write a final letter to yourself, forgiving yourself for any negativity you have carried. Forgive yourself for any mistakes you've been torturing yourself over, any unmet goals, unresolved resolutions, whatever you're carrying that weighs you down. Sending these letters is optional: Let your own heart decide, as the challenge in this is to purge your own heart of the anger you may have been carrying, but I encourage it. After all, compassion is the outward projection of those well wishes, that loving-kindness.

beyond // Forgiving others is a challenge, but asking for forgiveness can be the most humbling and intensely difficult thing we do. When faced with our own mistakes, especially those projected onto someone else, our every instinct is to avoid the consequence, avoid the fallout. This is unfair to every person involved, unfair to ourselves and our own personal growth, but mostly unfair to those affected by whatever our actions, or inactions, may have caused. Now is the time to set down that weight, and to allow them the same grace. Write an apology letter to someone you feel you have hurt. Write this honestly, write it plainly and free from excuses. Sometimes sorry is for the sayer, relieving the burden for only the person offering the apology, sometimes it is not. This is one of those times. Write this, send this, and expect nothing in return.

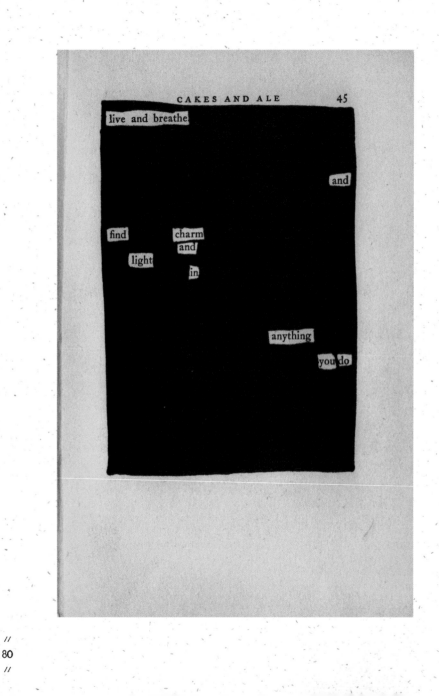

choice:
the enemy
of creativity?

A few years back, I began a writing exercise that I had dabbled with before but completely forgot about until I saw the brilliant Austin Kleon resurrecting. This was blackout poetry, and it was, and remains, an extremely helpful tool that I use for inspiration, for creative jump-starting, and for simplicity. To explain it briefly, it involves taking a page from an old book, a newspaper, or any piece of writing and, with a marker or pen, blacking out all but the words you wish to remain, creating a new poem or piece of work out of random individual words, scattered across the page. Reducing the many down to a few and, in the process, simplifying and beginning again. For all of us English-speaking folk, there are (according to most) about a quarter of a million words. That's 250,000 words we can sift through, play with, choose from, and write down. This is massively overwhelming and can often be a reason why people steer clear of writing. The sheer volume of usable words, the abundance of choice, can make actually choosing one seem like an insurmountable task. Unlimited choice can often be one of the biggest enemies of creativity, and blackout poetry reduces all that. Now you have at your disposal only the words that were already on the page. Now you are limited.

challenge // Find a book that is falling apart, find one that has been abandoned, destroyed, and is on the way to either the trash or the recycling bin. Choose a page from the book at random and tear it out. Next, grab a Sharpie marker. Any size will do, but I prefer the extra-fine point for the initial blocking, and then the chisel tip to finish the page. Create a new poem out of the limited words you are given. Do so by selecting the words that tell your new story and blacking out the rest. This is your poem, this is your creativity carved out of the words on the page. Think of each page as a slab of fresh marble. Your job is to slowly chisel out something new. There are no rules to this. You can write as short or as long a poem as you wish, just make sure you take only words and never phrases. Phrases belong to the original author, but the words belong to us all.

beyond // Can we find poetry in unconventional places?
Just like this book, sometimes we have to look in mundane places for
the most miraculous things. This beyond is to create another blackout
poem, but this time using completely nonpoetic sources. It's easy to
find beautiful words and poetry in exquisitely written old novels. What
is extremely difficult, however, is finding beautiful poems inside of en-
cyclopedias, science journals, or old manuals. Somehow, however, the
poetry we create from these feels different, more like an accomplish-
ment, perhaps even richer. Try this, you will see.

I cannot breathe
thinking of the roads
to come. The rain soaked cobbles,
the dirt and gravel
leading off into a something
I've not yet imagined.
Where do we put the
lust for the wander,
where do we keep it,
where can it grow, without
overgrowing the rest?
I am in love
with being this
breathless.

tourist in your own town

This world is a beautiful one, filled with more stunning sights than we'll ever be able to see in our lifetime. Mark Twain once said, "Travel is fatal to prejudice, bigotry, and narrow-mindedness," and I couldn't agree more. I make it a habit to encourage everyone I meet to find their way as far outside their comfort zone as possible, and often. This time, however, I'm encouraging something a little different. We see this world so often nowadays as the photographs we like from travel photographers on social media. We convince ourselves that the only way to find beauty like that is to travel far from home to these frequented locations in exotic locales. If we cannot go to the waterfalls in Iceland, see the northern lights in Norway, or visit the perfect beaches of the Caribbean, then why go anywhere at all? We forget, and we forget this often, that we all live in a place worth visiting—yes, all of us. Sometimes we need to see our homes in new light, or at the very least shine a new light on all the old haunts. We must pretend we are new and fresh, and our town has yet to be painted with our own eyes. We must seek out, and seek out with enthusiasm. We do not need to hop on a flight across the oceans, we do not need to spend huge sums of money to disappear into somewhere on the opposite side of the planet to find beauty. It's here, in front of us, and always has been.

challenge // A simple challenge, this, but a crucial one. For this challenge, you'll get to experience not the "tour" that you've probably given dozens of people who have visited you in your town, but rather all the spots off the beaten track. Quite simply: Be a tourist in your own town. Part of finding inspiration everywhere is to stop thinking you have to go somewhere to find it. Become your own cartographer and draw a basic map of your wandering, only instead of just visiting the famous landmarks, wander wide, wander far, and mark ordinary beauty, miniature miracles, emotional epiphanies, or serendipitous interactions you find along the way. Fill your map with as many details as you wish, but SEE your home as if you've never once visited it, as if you just stepped off the airplane with a blank itinerary and hours to kill. Look at the old and make it new.

beyond // For this beyond, all you have to do is leave five small tokens or treasures in your five favorite places you mapped for the next wanderer to discover and enjoy. Tiny discoveries like this can alter the course of a bad day, truly, so why not set someone else up for a little joy?

Spin softly through
my days,
twirl, dancer slow
and grace soaked.
I want to see
you waltz
across the face
of my
memories;
I want to carry them
as far as I
can go.

dance. dance. dance.

There is such art in letting go, such poetry in refusing to hold on so tightly to the constructs we spent so long creating. There is beauty in motion, in forgetting to care and curate our behavior, in losing ourselves in music, in song. Of all the prompts and challenges in this book, this one may be the toughest (for some of you), and might make you feel the silliest, the most vulnerable. For reasons that are tough to nail down, inhibition seems to grow like a fungus in our lives, spreading without our knowledge, covering our passions and joy and obscuring them from ourselves. We forget our own capacity for silly, untethered, hilarious joy, and sometimes it takes a little coaxing to bring it back out, to remind ourselves that we're capable of it. It's time to rid ourselves of this mold, to allow complete and ridiculous fun.

challenge //

As I said, this, by far, might be the most challenging of all the prompts inside this little book. As we age, we begin to lose our ability and desire to be childlike. We fear that acting this way is no longer acceptable, is no longer allowed. Creativity, true and lasting creativity, requires a heavy dose of childlike innocence and imagination. Therein lies the rub. Your challenge, should you choose to accept it: Turn on your favorite music and dance. Hard. Allow yourself to get lost in your dancing and don't worry who can see, who cares, or anything beyond your movement. Once you're sweaty and exhausted, pause and reflect with simple words, to yourself or to the wide world around you: What is holding you back from being your most authentic and childlike self? How do you feel your creativity could expand if you lost these inhibitions?

Don't worry, you don't have to share videos or photographic proof of your dancing with the world, but I'd love it if you did.

beyond // I know I've already asked you to do way more than you could have ever bargained for with the dancing challenge, but this time we're going to raise the bar just a tad higher. You're going to dance again, oh yes, but this time it's going to be a little more, well, visible. Here we go: Put your favorite headphones on, and yes, do this again . . . in public. As always, this is optional, but it is such a fantastic exercise on truly losing the inhibitions to finally to take life less seriously.

How tender can you be,
how delicate
with the thin glass
of another's
heart?

So many
with hammers for hands,
so few
can hold us.

clean your slate

Fewer things are more dangerous to our own discoveries in this life than preconceived notions. Fewer things limit our capacity for compassion, for curiosity, for spontaneity than coming into a situation with half-formed beliefs about things we may not have any actual knowledge about. Yet this happens and happens often. We meet people for the first time filled with opinions and ideas, judgments and biases that are created inside us based on information we've received from friends, colleagues, family members, or rumor. Sometimes, we tell ourselves, this is a good thing. Sometimes it may be, but often, this does nothing but distort the truth that we're supposed to find on our own, with our own experiences. We come to people with a dirty slate, a chalkboard filled with white powdered streaks, half-erased thoughts, pictures, and ideas. We, in short, bring our own sand to the beach. Doing this can skew our understanding of the person or situation in question. Doing this limits our ability to be compassionate and open-minded, and before we know it, we can talk ourselves out of what could be a new friendship, or at the very least, a new perspective on something we thought we understood, and understood well. I am completely and entirely aware that there are circumstances in our lives when our presuppositions offer advance warning and caution, and indeed keep us safe. The idea of cleaning the slate doesn't mean we should ignore every warning of every person who could potentially do us harm. Instead, it's that we should keep an open mind when meeting people who may have fallen out of favor with those who know them, with people we have no reason to dislike but are told to do so.

challenge // As the heading for this challenge recommends, clean your slate. Take the time to sort through the judgments and opinions you've been given by outside influences, that you've borrowed from others, and decide which truly deserve to stay. Are there people you've been avoiding based on rumor, unsolicited advice, or warnings of others? Are there places you've not visited based on opinions you've never validated for yourself? We limit ourselves far too often, refusing to try to connect with people, places, situations, foods, or ideas because they were labeled by someone, somewhere, as taboo, as off-limits. The brilliant ecologist Garrett Hardin once said: "It takes five years for a willing person's mind to change. Have patience with yourself and others when treading in an area protected by a taboo." If this is the case, then there is no better place to start than here, no better time than now. There is nothing wrong with being protective of your own heart, but when we allow ourselves to be controlled by unsubstantiated claims, we're missing too much of life and all it has to offer us. Learn for yourself what is worth keeping in your life, what is worth adding to it, what needs to go away. Clean your slate and allow everything to prove to you, for themselves, where they belong.

beyond // My best buddy, singer-songwriter Gregory Alan Isakov, once sang, "If it weren't for second chances, we'd all be alone." This is one of my favorite lines of his, and something that resonates profoundly in my life. This beyond challenge is about second chances. Sometimes it is impossible to have a perfectly clean slate for people who have, in fact, dirtied up our chalkboard with the dust of their actions. Sometimes we see the ghosted reminders of the words they've written, and it's hard to forget these. To go beyond, we can try to offer second chances to those who may have wronged us, may have pushed one too many buttons, may have betrayed or led us astray. We can go beyond for people we do not know but are fortified in a position that is so foreign to our own, people who hold beliefs we could never hold, people who come from different perspectives, offer different opinions, challenge our viewpoints in ways we are not used to experiencing. In no way should you let someone who has been harmful, abusive, or cruel to you back into your good graces, in no way should you ever put yourself in harm's way, in no way should you sacrifice your own convictions, but take a moment to figure out if there are people who have had minor indiscretions that you could forgive, and if so, do so. Grudges are heavy weights to carry, and sometimes the kindest thing we can do for ourselves is set them down.

I'll meditate on kindness
until I become it,
effortless and
true.
I'll practice love,
until I know nothing
but giving it.
Until I leak it
without ever
noticing.

a good deed
goes unposted

If a random act of kindness doesn't get videotaped "secretly" from a shaky and "hidden" mobile phone, uploaded to YouTube, shared across Instagram, Twitter, and Facebook, then broadcast to the *Today Show* and millions of people sharing a collective *Awwww*, did it even happen? When creating our children's book, *North Pole Ninjas*, Sarah Linden and I wanted to create a new holiday tradition that was based entirely on kindness, on a restructuring of the holiday season that aims at charity, at the act of giving without any expectation of receiving in return. In the book, we encourage kids to go out and perform secret "ninja" good deeds for neighbors, friends, or even strangers. We wanted to make sure that the motivation behind the actions in the story, behind the missions presented to the children and to their families reading it, were pure. We didn't want good deeds done for the praise, for the recognition and accolades; we wanted to remind people that the act itself is the reward, and no one, anywhere, needs to hear about it. We are in an oversaturated and over-curated society today. We share the highlights and leave out the shadows, we push for likes, for retweets, for followers, for acceptance and recognition, whether we like to admit it or not. This is a natural thing, this is understandable. The problem, as I see it, is the motivation behind the action, not the action itself. Regardless of our intentions, when we're motivated by those enticing and addictive positive reinforcements, the actual effect of doing a good deed is short-lived and fleeting. When this happens, the motivation to perform these acts of kindness then fades, fades, and finally stops. This is the tragedy, this is the reality I hope to avoid altogether. If we shift this, reorient our kindness toward the outward projection of it, not the hoped-for reward, the effect of those actions is elongated, stretched out and encompassing. No longer does the feeling fade, but rather it lasts, lingering long after our random act has been completed, just long enough for us to begin again and perform another. We can have seamless joy from this. All we have to do is give, and give, and give again.

challenge //

There is no time limit on giving, there is no best time to begin. What I would like is for "sometime" to become now, and so I want to challenge you. Today, decide upon a few random acts of kindness that inspire you, that wake you up and plant a seed of compassion that you want to see grow. This can be anything. This can be done anywhere. You don't have to pay off someone's entire Walmart layaway bill, nor do you have to work at a soup kitchen for the next week. You can do anything as long as it is kind, aimed with compassion, and feels necessary to you. Do this act, these acts, without any memorialization, without any photographs, without any sharing of any kind of the act being completed. And even more, do them anonymously, from start to finish. Like our North Pole Ninjas, hide the fact that you are doing these acts, and let the satisfaction you receive be enough. I promise, it is enough. Reframing the way we see kindness like this can also reframe the way we approach compassion in our lives: less a thing to be rewarded for, more a thing to be done because there is no other way.

beyond // Make this a habit you refuse to break. Choose one day each month to be your official Random Act of Kindness Day. Pick a number that means something to you, and symbolically name that day as such. Refuse to forget this day, refuse to become too busy or committed to skip it, and create a new ritual. If, after a few months go by, one day feels like too little, add another. Then another. Then another. This feeling is an addictive one, and before you understand how it happened, random acts of kindness will start happening every single day, without fail. No one but you will know, and it's magic this way. You'll see.

Birds got a name for it,
a murmuration,
when they, as many,
are one.
We need one too,
something to call ourselves
when we fight together
against the descent
into what we know we
should not be.
We need a name,
but first,
we need to take our many
and become
one.

find the middle ground

To say that we're living in polarizing times is an understatement of gigantic proportions. Whether we like to admit it openly or not, we are divided in so many ways, facing off instead of facing forward together. We protest, and then we protest the protests, and at the heart of it all is belief. These beliefs are often so fundamentally held, so intrinsic to who we are as people, that backing down and opening our minds can be a task too large for the asking. We hold our ground, they hold their ground, and the tug-of-war continues, no one ever winning, no one ever giving an inch to the other. While this is often an incredibly good thing, and I fully support standing up for your beliefs and holding tightly to what you believe is right and wrong, I also believe that one of the most important characteristics a person can have is to always remain open-minded. When we keep our minds open to opposing viewpoints, it allows us to see a fully framed picture of the situations we're dealing with, it allows us to grow, and it allows us to stand even firmer on the ground we know is under our own feet. Refusing this, closing off our minds to the views of others, only alienates us from one another further, it pushes everyone else back, and builds a giant wall instead of a bridge that may one day be crossed. Today, in this volatile and often frightening world, we need so many more bridges, and we need so many fewer walls. Keeping an open mind, trying to truly understand where others are coming from, is instrumental in finding and celebrating the underlying humanity that unites us all, as different as we may seem. We are all in this together, all passengers aboard the same spinning blue ship, and the sooner we realize this, the better.

challenge //

Is open-mindedness something we can practice? Can we cultivate a skill in patiently broadening our mental horizons and allowing in thoughts and beliefs that are counter to our own? I like to think so. I firmly believe that, while not easy, actively opening your mind is something that requires a great deal of practice, a great deal of mental exercise to get the appropriate muscle involved at the proper strength. It takes a lot of repetition, a lot of patience and energy, but it is possible. I want you to try, too. The challenge here is to seek out someone who holds an opinion or concrete belief system that is contrary to how you feel about a particularly polarizing subject. Ask them if they'd be willing to talk, tell them you have questions and are actively trying to learn and understand viewpoints that run antithetical to your own. When with this person, or people, listen. Ask intelligent questions, without a hint of judgment or bias, and truly listen. People are passionate creatures, holding on dearly to the things they have been taught, have come to believe, and what they know. Often, this is a beautiful thing. Often, it can be overwhelming and frightening. Here is your chance to fully hear and begin to understand the other side, whatever side that may be. In no way feel you need to change your own beliefs in this exercise, and in no way feel like you need to argue your belief during this process—it's not about that. This is about keeping an open mind and allowing yourself to stretch your own capacity for understanding and patience. I have a sneaking suspicion that your own beliefs will be solidified after your meetings, that you will believe with new vigor and conviction, and that is just fine. If we all just met in the middle a little more often, even mentally, even for a time, we would reap countless benefits.

beyond // In this beyond challenge, I want you to test the waters with the person or people you had your conversation with and ask if they would be willing to listen to your side, just as patiently, just as openly, as you listened to theirs. If they agree, tell them how you came to end up where you did in your belief system, why you hold it still, and how you feel when discussing it, how you felt hearing theirs. Actively try to find common ground that you both can agree upon, points where you can say you see eye to eye. We hold a misconception that because someone stands on the other side of an issue, there is absolutely no common ground, absolutely no way anything is shared between you. This is often catastrophically wrong, and believing that we cannot reach across these lines only divides us further. If we can have intelligent discourse in a situation like this, we can have it anywhere, with anyone, at any time, and who knows how much more progress we can enjoy. We have to start somewhere to close some of these divides. Perhaps it needs to start here, start with us.

You're not gonna want to hear this,
but I'll say it
anyway:
it's the sad days, the long ones that
feel like they'll never end,
that reveal the person
buried beneath
all that charade.
It's the sorrow that shapes us,
the heartache,
and how we respond.
We are created
by what we
endure.

earn it

I'm going to be blunt here, as I have been from time to time in this little book. I'm going to be blunt and I'm going to do so in the form of a quote from a book I love, *Fight Club* by Chuck Palahniuk: "You are not special. You're not a beautiful and unique snowflake. You're the same decaying organic matter as everything else. We're all part of the same compost heap. We're all singing, all dancing crap of the world." As harsh as this may sound, there is something absolutely beautiful about the truth behind it. While we all are unique, each adding layers upon layers onto the people, the personalities we become, when broken down, we're all the same, and we're all doing our best. We run into problems when we believe we are entitled to things we've not yet earned. Chief among these: respect. The instant-gratification nature of our society has at times created an epidemic of people believing they are entitled to any number of things, without the people having done anything to actually earn this entitlement. We believe we are entitled to high-paying jobs that require no effort simply because we want them. We believe we're entitled to leisure without the work that pays for it, to respect and admiration even if we've not done much to aim that spotlight in our direction. We are so accustomed to receiving what we want when we want it that we forget sometimes what is actually involved in the process of receiving it. In this book, I would like anyone who reads it, including myself as I type these words, to understand that harsh truths are often the keys to unlock the doors keeping us from becoming the people we're supposed to become, that keep us from seeing the world how we could be seeing it, full of beauty and light. Understanding that we too fall prey to this condition is instrumental in getting over it, and in seeing ourselves with fresh eyes, unadorned and open to the life around us.

challenge //

Put simply, earn it. Take that long, hard, honest look at yourself and, without sugarcoating or viewing through rose-colored glasses, admit the areas you've been expecting things without putting in the work to earn them. Search out any behavior of entitlement, admit it, and address it. The first step in recovering from a problem is admitting that there is one. By admitting that we often demand things from life, be it respect, stability, entertainment, or understanding, without truly putting in the time and energy to earn them, we can begin to move forward toward a more mindful, more present, connected, and happier future. This newly adopted mindfulness can carry us into the next chapters of our lives with a clarity we've not yet known.

Make a list of the things you find that you want or need most in life. This doesn't necessarily need to be a list of goals, just things your life has been lacking. Make this list, fold the paper in half, and on the opposite side, make a list of what you'll need to do in order to achieve them. What do you have to put into this to get out of it what you believe you are entitled to? Nothing comes easy, this much is true, but great things most of all demand effort, respect, and attention. What do you have in you that can lead to these things? Seeing it spilled out and outlined in front of us can be the reminder we need, the push we've been waiting for, to truly begin.

beyond // Instead of looking forward at all the things you want and need as you did in the challenge, now look back at all the things you've already been given, and in doing so, highlight all the things you earned and all the things you were given freely without earning them. Whenever you find something on this list that you received, show appreciation. Write letters, emails, messages, or make phone calls to those who helped you get to where you are now; show them the respect *they* deserve for helping you before you earned the respect they so freely gave. Admitting the help we had along the way is a huge and fundamental part of understanding that we are the combination of so many different parts and pieces, that it's always work and effort that lead to it, whether that is our effort or someone else's.

If I do not follow you
out of this zone of comfort
I've lived safely inside,
Push me, pull me, or
throw me from that
circle. If my wander loses
its lust, if the soles of my feet
begin to rust, if I forget
the way to adventure,
force it upon me until I
remember; demand a life
five thousand shades
from ordinary.

branch out

Routine can be a beautiful thing, a comforting blanket that wraps us up in familiarity and brings a level of comfort and security that can be really challenging to abandon. It can also be the assassin of our creativity, locking us into the grooves we've worn into our lives. Shaking this up can be tough. It can feel foreign and alienating, it can make us feel weak, vulnerable, and completely out of our element. What a gift that is. I've long believed that our full potential is always lingering, loitering around and hoping we'll notice, just beyond that zone of comfort we've all allowed ourselves to call home. Sometimes we must run, shouting or singing, skipping or kicking, just beyond those borders, and find a place to plant another of our flags. Oddly, it's doing precisely this that leads to the greening of the grass we left behind. I believe the soil we know so well is only enriched by leaving it from time to time, seeing new things, experiencing something vastly different, and then returning with an appreciation freshly blossomed.

challenge // How do we ever get out of our comfort zones if we do not take the plunge? How do we grow in our own art forms if we do not wander? All I wish you to do is jump, leap, skip, hop, fumble, or, if you must, fall kicking and screaming into an art form of any kind that is not your own. You do not need to take a course or pay for lessons or anything of the sort, simply attempt an art form that you've always been attracted to but never really attempted. Do not try to do this as anyone other than yourself, do not try to reach some unobtainable goal, do not worry even about the final product, as the practice itself is the goal. Whichever you choose, immerse yourself in the spirit of creation—smell the paints, feel the textures of the clay, listen closely to the sound of graphite on paper, hear the instruments you play and the echo in the silent moments; whatever you are working on, be all the way there, fully present, and give it the respect and honest effort it deserves. Find the bits of beauty that comprise something that was previously unknown to you. Once you've completed this, reflect on the experience, and write or speak or even just think about how it is similar to the form of creativity that comes most naturally to you, then write, speak, or think about how it is different. Are there elements you can borrow to make you better at your own?

beyond // It's tough jumping out of your comfort zone, it's tough trying something you're not already good at, but it stretches us, and stretching is wonderful. What can be even more of a challenge is jumping back into your own comfort zone, but doing it in a whole different way. Dive back into your own chosen form of creativity, but switch things up and do it in a way you never have before. Into watercolor painting? Try oils. Try cattle markers, try acrylics. Always write poetry? Try short stories, try long prose. Whatever art form you choose, switch it up, sing new notes, make new art, just force yourself out of the box. It's beautiful out here.

Ever feel crushed by the weight
of the places you need
to see?
Flattened out by the big round
world that keeps spinning
while you sit, still?
Split me in a million parts
and plant each somewhere
new. Let me grow
in a million spots,
let me call them
home.

darts

We've all played the game where we take a globe, spin it as fast as
we can, lightly place our fingertip atop it, and see where we end
up. We promise ourselves: One day, we'll go. One day, we'll find
our way to those strange distant shores, we'll see what magic lives
there. Our young imaginations run away with us on those days, im-
ages are invented in our minds, pictures of how it could possibly
look, what lives could possibly fill it. We invent stories, we invent
sunsets, we invent drama and action and adventure. We lift our fin-
gers, and we're still standing in the same place, but somehow we
know, we left. And we will go again. Travel is so fundamentally im-
portant to who we are as people, and so vital to understanding the
tapestry of this human condition, that I want to encourage it and
encourage it often. Stoking that fire of exploration in ourselves is
something that must be done, as so much of our imagination lives
in curiosity, in adventure, in removing ourselves from our comfort
zones, and finding ourselves along the way.

challenge // Do not worry, you won't be spinning a globe in this challenge. Well, not exactly. This is the grown-up version, and as we're probably mostly grown-ups, we're clearly going to be using darts. And maps. Since I know that travel is expensive and not always feasible given the demands of our lives, our jobs, our commitments, and our budgets, I won't ask you to empty out your calendars or your pocketbooks to make this challenge one you can complete. Here's what I will ask you to do: Grab a map of your state (or, if you're reading this internationally, your country) and lay it out flat or hang it up on the wall, but please make sure it's not a wall you mind sticking a hole through. Find a dart, or if you don't have a dart, find a pen, pencil, or marker that can substitute. Walk a few paces back, spin yourself around, open your eyes, and throw. Wherever that dart (or pen, pencil, or marker mark) lands, make yourself this promise, and give it a deadline: You will go, and soon. Plan a road trip, or day trip depending on how big your state or country is, to whatever bit of visitable earth the dart landed near. Pack your camera, pack your journal, pack yourself, and go, and when you go, write about what you find. Photograph the perfect adventure you throw yourself into. Find that spark of wanderlust reignited, and remember the way your imagination used to fuel it, the way it still can. This spark needs our oxygen to burn, and somewhere along the way we forgot to feed it.

beyond // How do you take this a step further? How can we revisit that globe-spinning, dart-throwing, wanderlust-fueled wonderment we once lived in? Simple, really. Now is the time to take this challenge truly beyond, by tossing aside the state or country map and spinning that globe of this beautiful blue marble we're all living on. Find a world map and re-create the challenge you just completed. Or if you have one, find the globe and spin it, lightly hovering your fingertip above it. Wherever the dart lands, wherever your finger stops, go. It doesn't have to be now, it doesn't have to be five years from now, but put that spot on your bucket list and make yourself promise that one day, you will go. Keep this seed, this spark, burning in the back of your mind, and save a little every month, every year, until you can go. Find yourself reminded of the wide, wild world we've been gifted, and let your imagination aim at this far-off place, no matter how long it takes to find yourself there. In the meantime, write something, anything, about what it may be like when you finally go. Write about those beautiful images that rush through your brain as you imagine a life there. Write about what it will take to get there, what it will take to finally arrive. This is a bucket-list item you never intended on adding, and now, it may be one of your most mysterious, your most fun.

This is the passing
of a cloud,
this is a bird
sent wandering.
This is the coffee
in your cup,
this is my hand
on your thigh.

Everywhere,
wonder.

notice
everything

At the root of creativity, I've always believed, is curiosity. Whatever the art form you practice, whatever the manifestation of your creativity, the more curiosity and creation will grow. For me, this curiosity is most easily accessed, this flame most readily fanned, by simply noticing. Notice everything. Eyes and ears open, the world seems to open up, like sight restored after a lifetime of blindness. If we begin practicing truly *noticing*, it becomes second nature, it becomes the way we wander through every day, not a challenge we have to set for ourselves, not a way of life we've always envied in someone else. What we forget is that we can cultivate this, we can truly practice it, get better at it, and see more. There is so much out there, so much hiding, waiting. It's up to us to open our eyes, to challenge our senses, to see it all.

challenge // By now, you've been practicing seeing the world in a deeper, richer, and more positive light, and might be finding it a bit more natural and second nature. Show us. All of us. You may not call yourself a photographer, and this is fine, we don't mind. Using whatever camera and equipment you may have at your disposal, be it a fancy DSLR, an old-fashioned film camera, or even just your smartphone, take ten photographs of ordinary things from an ordinary day that you may have never noticed until today. These photographs do not have to be National Geographic quality, they don't have to be billboard resolution or hashtag worthy on Instagram. They don't have to be of anything specific, they don't have to follow any photography rules, they don't have to be anything other than beautiful to you. Beauty is hiding absolutely everywhere, disguised as the mundane, hidden beneath layers of overlooked and underappreciated haze. Find them, unearth them, and make them into the art they've always been. Art, true art, is in the eye of the beholder. Use your training to behold it in ways you didn't know you could.

beyond // Sometimes, as a challenge and prompt to myself, I will try to write poetry or short stories based on photographs I've taken, or even sometimes, photographs I have seen. I try to immerse myself in that frozen moment, the world that revolves around it, and get lost there. Your beyond is to write a story or poem about one of your photographs. Go into as much detail as you wish, but dive right in. Illuminate the world that exists frozen in that tiny snapshot. The beauty, the drama, the wonder that fills it.

Strength speaks
in a hundred voices,
begins with a hundred faces.
Sometimes it shouts, sometimes
it demands.
Some strength is born
as a whisper, a lullaby sang
in the face of it all;
some strength disguises itself
as kindness, as the unafraid giving
of all that is had.
This strength is that strength,
the pour, when others drink,
the steady, where some may
shake.
This strength is a quiet one,
a soundless roar that needs not
the quivering in return.
this strength is,
and always has been.

make them everything

Few personality traits carry an inherent grace like the ability to make each person you meet or speak with feel like they are the only person in the room, the only person on the planet. That they, exactly as they are, are appreciated and respected, worthy of being noticed. There is such an intense kindness to this, such a fascinated curiosity, such a simple gift. When we listen, truly listen, not just with our ears and eyes but with our hearts and with our compassion and understanding, it acts like a key to the lock on the door between people. It opens a connection that cannot be manufactured, and cannot be faked. Such truths tumble out when we make people feel this way, such intimacy created, such security, and these are things we are all so desperate for. We all want to feel vital, if for a moment, in the life of someone else. We all want to feel like we are heard, and more, understood. When I think of the person I want to be, the traits I most want to exhibit, I keep going back to this, time and time again. This is the target I'll keep aiming at, and I cannot help believing that if everyone else did as well, things might be a lot different than they are now.

challenge // It should come as no surprise that the challenge in this is to aim at the target of making each and every person feel appreciated, feel adored, feel noticed and respected. More, to try and try and try again to make this a habit you'll never break, a norm you'll adopt. On the surface, this does not sound that monumentally difficult, and this sounds like simply making those important genuine connections that opened this very book, but the pace and demands of our lives can often make this one of the first things on the chopping block. Those genuine connections can fall by the wayside after the first day attempting them. We check our phones while being told a story, we have the television on while conversing on the phone, we forget to listen, we forget to hear. Somewhere along the way, we've begun losing our ability to truly be present with the people we interact with, and what a heartbreaking reality this is. For the next day, just to start, force yourself to be entirely present, engaged, and interested in each person you speak with. Do not do this as a charade or a facetious front. Do it honestly, and do it with purpose and purity. While listening, study them, appreciate the intricacies that make them who they are, and feel no fear in pointing out to them the things that impress you, that interest you, that you respect. Watch how the people in your life change, watch how the depth of your conversations changes, watch how their trust, their vulnerability, their connection, grows. When the day is up, add another, and then another, and then another. Make this change a permanent one, and watch how that personality trait becomes one you are defined by. This is a transformative thing, and it's abundantly clear it's long overdue.

beyond // Part of becoming the things we wish to become is in discovering where we may be falling short. In the attempt to make each person we interact with feel important, feel like the only one in the room, we must first ask in what ways we can improve. Ask people you interact with, speak to, live with, or see on a regular basis whether they consider you a good listener, whether they consider you someone they can trust and come to with important things in their lives. Ask them for advice on how you could be better at those things, how you could improve and make them feel more noticed, appreciated, and understood. Then think of someone in your life who you would already describe this way, someone who has made you feel this or continues to make you feel this, and ask them how they do it. Ask what they feel when speaking to people, what they've learned along the way. Listen, and change.

Let it pass through me, let
it all pass through;
I am the valley
and these words,
the river.
Let me know what I say
only after it's been said,
typed and released
to the air, to the
winds that carry us.
I am carved by
what I've written,
and I have written
what I know.

be a conduit,
not a conductor

Why do we think we're capable of controlling everything? When does this belief bleed into our lives, when does it stain the tapestry of our days? We focus so much attention on trying to control every aspect of our daily lives that it spills over into our creativity, into the way we perceive things, and this often happens without us noticing. When this misguided belief on control does leak into our creative processes, it can so drastically alter not only our productivity, but our originality. The more we try to corral and restrict the thoughts that naturally want to form, the more we censor our own internal dialogue. I firmly believe that if we do this enough we can silence the voice that has existed in us since before we could articulate it, before we could form it into understandable mediums. For children, and for myself living as someone on the autism spectrum, these vital thoughts come in without censorship or sorting, without rhyme, reason, or any semblance of order, and they come in often. I've never had the capacity to channel them, and as such, my creative output has always maintained a strangely high level without the restraint of control. This led me to the conduit/conductor philosophy I hold on to pretty dearly and bring up often to people who ask for advice on writer's block or any form of creative block they may be dealing with. If we allow ourselves to shift out of the conductor role, put down the batons and flow into a conduit role, things change and change drastically. By seeing ourselves as nothing more than the vessel creativity must pass through, we remove the hurdles it must leap over and allow it to flow freely and unrestricted. Who knows what we can create when we stop trying to control our creativity?

challenge // Our minds are busy and chaotic creatures. They move when we wish they wouldn't, they quiet and are wordless when we most need them to speak up. This is a question I am asked almost more than any other: How do you overcome writer's block and find words again? A tough challenge in our lives is to stop fighting our thoughts and to start making them work *for* us. Try this on for size: For fifteen straight minutes, write or type, without any worry of grammar or punctuation, all the thoughts that find their way into your head. Let them pass through you, and treat yourself as a conduit, not a filter. You are the vessel, so allow the words to pour out however they will. For the first time, feel yourself *channeling* them instead of *searching* for them. Once you've done this, take note of what you wrote, take note of where your thoughts traveled to naturally, of the way you captured them, and remember this anytime you feel stuck, blocked, or unable to create.

beyond // This is an exercise I complete often for no other reason than to sink deeper into the random worlds our minds create. Try this: Take one of your most profound random thoughts from this challenge and expound upon it. Write about it in greater depth and clarity, and find truth hiding in what your brain created on its own. Sometimes the voice inside knows much more than we give it credit for, passing its thoughts off as random and insignificant. No longer.

What if all we are
is the combination
of all we have seen
and all our hands
have ever closed upon?
We are the ticket stubs
and lucky coins,
the falling stars
and the sound
a voice makes
as its song comes
to a haunting close
in a crowded hall.
The weathered rocks
in dark pockets and
the torn fragments
of our favorite books.
We are the pieces
of all we have ever found
glued tight inside us,
shining out.

chase joy with wild abandon

What's the point of this? Honestly, what's the point of our brief lap around this lifetime? We spend hours upon hours doing so many things we think we *should* be doing that we forget the point. You've read it, you've heard it said much more eloquently than I could probably say it here, but we spend a life working and waiting for some eventual happiness, some faraway joy we think we have to struggle to reach, and by the time we get there, we're exhausted, worn out and worn down, and pushing it off even further. *Tomorrow* is simultaneously one of the most hopeful and horrible words. If we spend all these hours waiting for tomorrow, how much do we miss in the meantime? Ralph Waldo Emerson once wrote, "How much of human life is lost in waiting!" How much, indeed?

Joy, unbridled and wildly chased, does not exist in this mythical land of tomorrow. Joy is now, the present moment saturated with fleeting and ephemeral beauty, if only we allow ourselves to see it. We've become so preoccupied in this misguided belief that there are rules that must be obeyed, respect given to the delaying of happiness, that we miss the whole point of this, the answer to the questions we keep asking. What happens when we chase joy— wildly, passionately, and with reckless abandon? What happens when we allow ourselves the indignity of celebrating it, looking silly while doing so, and truly enjoying each moment of each day? Happiness is temporary. It fades, ebbing often and returning randomly, but joy is something different entirely. Joy stays.

challenge // Take back today. Call in sick to school, take the day off from work, cancel your appointments, shut off your phone, and *live*. Do whatever things make you feel joyful, and do them all day long. We've all heard the phrase "Treat yourself," and now is the time to put it into action. Take a day for yourself, go to the movies, read the book you've been waiting to read, eat the foods you love, explore the places you want to see, go on the date, do whatever you want and need to do to feel joy pulse through you. These can be small things, they can be minor changes, but make joy your target, your aim. Take the day for yourself and feel no guilt in doing so. Life is short. What is the point of all this if we don't stop sometimes and truly enjoy? So much of human life IS lost in waiting, but not today. Not this time.

beyond // How do you take this challenge to a place beyond? Simple. This one I am going to give a little disclaimer for: This is not for the fainthearted, this is not to be done on a whim, but it is to be done if you qualify for it. The beyond challenge here is to do, or stop doing, something that has been acting as a constant roadblock to your joy. Miserable at your job? Put in your two weeks' notice after looking— *today*—for a replacement. In a relationship that is all give and no return? Stop. Stop allowing yourself to put off your own joy because the fear of change is greater than the fear of misery. Buy the plane tickets, plan the trip, change your life in all the ways you've desperately wanted to but have been too paralyzed to do so. It's time, today. Tomorrow is ages away.

However you are,
no matter how you were,
or began as,
however you are,
now,
is how you should be,
how we love you.
It matters not
what you call yourself,
what they call you,
what label, what
name,
you are perfect
this way,
this way.

old-fashioned love letters

When did love letters, true and honest old-fashioned love letters, fall out of favor? Emails replaced letters, text messages replaced emails, and now, a simple swipe on the screen and an emoji have replaced even the simplest text messages. Somewhere along the way we lost the method to telling those we love how we love them. In that, we've lost the way of telling ourselves that we love who we are. We are bombarded by holidays aimed at romance, at the idea that we always have to have someone to love, but it misses a step. It misses the simple and altogether cliché idea that we cannot truly love others until we understand how to love ourselves. Perhaps when we lost the ability to tell others, we lost sight of what it was in us that deserved the same acclaim. We look in mirrors and we see flaws; we're given compliments, but we only hear lies. We convince ourselves that our worth is based on being reminded of it from others despite never believing it when we do. We think ourselves lost, if alone, and forget the strength that has always existed inside us. What a catastrophe this is.

challenge // Many of us will be alone while reading this, many of us will be alone on any one of the many holidays aimed at love, at couple-hood, and as such, I'm going to allow something that might surprise you: a few moments of negativity. Write a list to yourself in which you point out everything you consider a flaw. These can be things you are negative about physically or personality-wise, but take a moment to pick yourself apart. Write as openly as you can, and let yourself emotionally respond to each and every thing you write down. The moment this list is done, fold it in half, and then fold it in half again. Now fold it in half once more. With your own two hands, tear it in half lengthwise. Take those pieces and tear them in half again. Do this for both halves of the original paper until all that's left are small pieces of hateful and negative confetti. Throw this high into the air and dance beneath it. Let it fall all around you, snowflakes of some perceived shortcomings, tiny fragments of the negative viewpoint you hold for yourself. Now with a new piece of paper, write yourself a love letter. A real, long, honest, old-fashioned love letter about everything that makes *you* special, that makes you magic and worthy of love. Have the courage to dig deep and allow yourself to truly celebrate everything that makes you unique and perfectly you. Here comes the hard part: Share it with us, with everyone, everywhere. Show US what you love about yourself, and let all of us fall in love too.

beyond // While we're reviving love letters, bringing back the forgotten art of slowly and beautifully expressing to ourselves all the things we cherish, we're going to take it a step further. Write a second letter to someone else who might need it, someone who may be feeling precisely how you felt before you began this exercise, someone who doesn't see themselves how you see them, how everyone probably does. Fill this letter with all you love about them, all the hidden things they don't think you see, the details that go beyond skin-deep, the personality traits, everything. Send this, deliver this, get this to them, and say nothing else. Your words will do the rest.

I'm chasing something,
always,
light is just the form
it usually takes,
I'm always running
straight at that feeling
when all else fades away
but what truly
matters.
Let it rise to me
like smoke
from a fire
freshly lit;
let it bathe me
in fog
and glow.

chase the light.
literally.

I speak often (okay, *often* is a bit of an understatement) about chasing the light. It was the name of my first book of poetry, it's the name of my photography business, it's who I am, who I've always been. Chasing the light is my mantra, my fundamental belief, my approach to all forms of creativity. I am a chaser of the light, and whether I'm taking photographs, writing poetry, or traveling, it's what I'm doing, always. This has created a shift in my perspective that has trickled into every aspect of my life, and I believe it will have the same effect on you. Chasing the light will be your vehicle to a new beginning, a way to open a door to your creativity.

challenge //

This challenge is an easy one, one that requires very little equipment but a great deal of creativity and possibly a little foot power. Using whatever camera you have—yes even your mobile phone will work—go on a light-hunting photo adventure. You can go anywhere, you can choose any time of day or night; the options are completely unlimited. Your only subject for the day needs to be the light, or often the lack thereof, in all its glory. Chase the light, chase the shadows it leaves behind, chase it and borrow it for a while in your photographs. Take as many photos as you wish, but allow yourself the space and freedom to wander, allow yourself the opportunity to see light as the subject instead of a factor on your subjects. You do not have to be a professional, your photos do not have to be gallery quality, I'm just encouraging you to see things, see light, in new ways, in new forms, and to open your eyes to all the different ways it shapes the day we wander through. Share the shine, share the shadows, and show everyone the way light has found you.

beyond// Not all light is literal, not all manifestations of it exist in the form we are most familiar with. Sometimes people can be light for us, sometimes they can embody so many of the characteristics you just spent an afternoon chasing. Now take your photography search a bit further. Take a photo of a person, or multiple people, who feel like the metaphorical representation of light to you. Stranger or friend, it doesn't matter, you're just looking for the light in the form of someone who feels like "light" to you. Once you've completed this, show them, and explain why they embody this for you.

Look twice at the eyes,
twice more at the smile,
for you know not what it hides,
what lives below, buried, that
the seam of smiling lips
can seal in. We all carry ache
in different ways, some with
swollen eyes and cheeks eroded
by tears, but others
with strong smiles and forced
laughter that sounds nothing
but authentic. Take the time to
sink below their surfaces,
those seconds, those precious
extra seconds, can completely
change a life.

the (sub)way forward

There are certain pieces of our lives that we never forget . . . first kisses, first dates, first failures, firsts. I will never forget my first trip to New York City. Growing up, I lived all over, in cities of all shapes and sizes, but somehow the Big Apple eluded me. When finally signing up for my first adventure into NYC, I had advice from people all over the great state of Montana ringing in my ears. The one piece that stood out the most made me a bit sad and a bit worried about the state of things. Everyone told me: "When taking the subway, don't make much eye contact, don't initiate any conversations, just keep to yourself, and everything will be great." If you know me at all, you'll know that I am rather rubbish at taking direction, and when arriving in New York, I promptly forgot every single thing that every single person advised me on. I remember my first trip to New York City, but mostly, I remember my first subway ride. I looked in every person's eyes, I started conversations with everyone around me, I asked questions, I listened, I laughed, and I connected. By the time I arrived at my stop, I had new friends, I had a new understanding of people who lived a life completely different from the one I knew.

challenge // Take a public transport journey that breaks every rule you may or may not have been taught. If you were never advised as I was, then take the advice I was given and completely disregard it. Find a subway, a bus, or a train and make connections. Ask questions, learn about the people who share the ride, and seek understanding. We're in a society that puts earbuds into our ear canals and drowns out the world, that avoids contact, that isolates people and retreats to the cool glow of our mobile devices. We are lonely because we're surrounded by people, but we never allow ourselves the grace of opening up, of welcoming strangers into our lives. During this challenge, speak less and listen more. Allow people to tell you their stories, why they ride that train, what they do, how they do it, who they are. Just listen, because everyone, everywhere, has a beautiful story to tell.

beyond // New routes lead to new stories. We humans are creatures of habit, and sometimes we need to shake things up to stretch our own boundaries. After you tackle this challenge, I'm going to switch things up and broaden your horizon even further. Take a new route on public transport: If you usually take a train, take a bus. If you usually take a cab, take the subway. If there's only one option, walk to a different stop and take that. Whatever you do, however you usually get to where you're going, try a different way, and with that, be introduced to a whole new group of people. Start again, learn their stories, make new connections with people who might be completely different from you . . . I think the biggest surprise will come in all the ways they are not so different from you—at all.

We forget to stop,
we forget to pay them
any mind,
and feel no remorse
in this forgetting.

Eyes closed,
we wander through this
life, we don't know
we've got honeycomb hearts
that need that
pollen.

Maybe if we knew,
if we all
just knew,
we'll all be back
as flowers.

in the moment

A consequence of traveling, and traveling a lot, is that you're often presented with a million memorable moments in a million memorable places. This is a blessing, quite obviously, yet over the last few years I have noticed something shift, both in myself and in the society that I'm a part of. I see so many amazing and beautiful photographs of places all around the world, and I am filled with wanderlust, of envy for those standing there. So I go. This is where the change takes place, this is the shift I am speaking of: Everywhere I go, there are people who are only halfway there at the very best. Often, myself included. I see people staring at four-inch screens instead of the 14,000-foot mountains beyond. I see people looking, eyes squinted and fingers ready, at their phones instead of toward the sunset unfolding. I see the slow rotation of coffee cups on wooden tables, the standing on chairs to photograph the meal. I see the uploading, while listening to conversation grind to a halt. I see halfway there, I see the other half lost in trying to share a curated moment rather than enjoying the one that's actually happening. A million memorable moments: How many of them are missed? It is unclear how this phenomenon leaked into our lives, when it first began shifting the way we approach the times that excite us or wake us up, but it can be worrisome. Why do we feel such a burning need to share every new thing that happens to us with people, many of whom we've never met? If we don't capture it, caption it, hashtag it, and spread it around the internet, does it lose value? We've become so busy trying to curate the perfect capture of a single second, we miss out on the live, in-person, ephemeral beauty that will never look this way again.

challenge// I am a photographer, so I will absolutely never tell you not to capture a moment you want to immortalize and keep. I will never tell you to let every moment pass by uncaptured, but I will say this: The exact next time you find yourself surrounded by something beautiful, resist—no, *ignore*—the urge to capture it. Let *this* one stay unstolen, unshared. Take a deep breath, and with every piece of yourself, be a witness to the beauty unfolding. See it. Truly see it. Let your other senses join, take note of the sounds that surround it, the smells, the way the air feels against your skin, the way you stay. We are always halfway there, and it's time we changed that. One less photo to share but, my goodness, so much to gain. Be there. All the way.

beyond // Capture it, but not now. Try this the next time you're faced with the infinitely Instagrammable: Follow through with this challenge, forgoing the urge to photograph it, to capture it and save it forever, and instead, memorize every single detail you possibly can. Study the scene, breathe it in completely, and save it all for later. When the moment passes, when you are home, when stillness finds you in the hours that will follow, re-create the scene in an art form of your choosing. If you wish, write about it in as much detail as you can muster, paint it, draw it, create a song for it, whatever you wish, but bring all those details back in a way you can save. We have within us an enormous capacity for the curating of these moments, these revelatory minutes; we just need to practice. Start here.

If you grow (and grow
you shall) to be one
(you will be one hundred
billion things) thing,
and one (out of all
the infinities stirring)
alone (you are never,
ever, alone), let it be
gentle.

observational meditation

We go through life often forgetting we are not the very center of the universe around us. We see ourselves as the sun, and everything else just a planet that orbits around the life we've carved out. This is a natural side effect of a life spent practicing survival, self-preservation, and learning to take care of ourselves, but nevertheless, it hides deeper truths. One tool I've used over the years to help rid myself of this incorrect and limiting viewpoint is meditation. I meditate on compassion, on kindness, on creativity, and often on this very point, this idea that we're not the center of all things but only one component. It sounds simple, it sounds obvious, but by directing our thoughts and our senses to this specific character misconception, it allows our minds to shift the narrative and expand into areas once closed off and forgotten.

challenge //

By practicing sitting meditation, with a direct emphasis on sound, even beginners can reap amazing benefits from the practice. It doesn't matter if you are a practiced meditation master or someone who has never once sat still for longer than three minutes, anyone can do this, and anyone can feel the effects. Sit, still and quiet, wherever you find yourself, and begin paying direct attention to the sounds closest to yourself. Focus on every sound you immediately notice, hear them, let them find their way into your consciousness. Now, settle further, and find the next layer of sounds farther outside yourself. Look for the ones beneath the surface-level sounds you've already noticed, the ones on the periphery, farther away and softer. Now go farther, finding sounds even more distant, the ones that are hard to hear, faint but there. See life as nothing more than giant circles, extending outward from where you are, all of them filled with life, with sound, all their own. Remember that to everyone else, you are just a sound in their meditation, whether you're nearby or so distant that you are a faint whisper. Layers upon layers of sound, with no center, only circles radiating out, encompassing everything. Open your eyes and describe the sounds you heard, beginning with the nearest and ending with the farthest away. Notice everything, and understand how you are only one small component of a much bigger life. Notice how your entire being feels calmer, more balanced, and yes, more centered.

beyond // While this challenge may indeed feel chal-
lenging for many of you, particularly those who have never attempted
any form of meditation, there is a way to take it further, to challenge
yourself beyond this, and in doing so to find an even deeper under-
standing. Try this exercise again, only this time, attempt it while in a
crowded place with lots of noise and commotion. First, try to find the
layers of sound, the circles that we're all a part of. Try to uncover the
most distant first, working your way back to the closest. It takes prac-
tice and it takes focus, but try all the same. In all of this, all of this sound
and understanding, try again to find the same levels of peace, of calm.

Hold these words in a book
and hold them close,
and I will try to make them
worthy.
These are trees,
these are leaves, and
branches fallen;
I will try to make
the forests
proud
of their reincarnation.

hidden
bookmarks

Two different art forms have, to me, always been paramount: music and books. Sharing these, allowing others to experience what moves me, what inspires me, what turns me on, has been just as important, just as vital. Both forms express things that other gifts cannot, and as such, both act not only as a gift, but a window into the gift giver, shining a light on what stirs their soul, what wakes them up, what brings them peace, or calm, or joy. With books in particular, our tastes can be so well defined that choosing a book as a gift can be absolutely revelatory. Truly, what we fall in love with, what we find beautiful, what we're inspired by says much about who we are. Showing this to others can make us feel vulnerable, but that vulnerability is staggeringly beautiful, and people deserve to know these pieces of ourselves. What if we could give these pieces of ourselves to others without them even knowing we're doing so? What if we could give discoveries to strangers, little windows into the soul of another, by leaving bits of ourselves behind? We can.

challenge // This challenge is a fun one, somewhat of a scavenger hunt in reverse. As we all know, finding hidden treasures, leftover notes, random bookmarks, front-cover dedications, and the lot can be a brief and tiny explosion of joy and understanding when buying a book, used or brand new. I cherish the heartfelt inscriptions hiding beneath the front cover of abandoned books, the tiny notes that hint at a giant life lived. Now it's our turn to create some of these for others to find. Write three short letters or notes to three people you will most likely never meet, with words of positivity, your favorite poem or quotation, or any advice you may have on happiness, love, or life, and fold them up small. Go to your favorite bookstore or library, and stealthily leave one letter in each of your three favorite books scattered somewhere on the shelves. This is a dose of kindness you will never see land, and in that, it makes it breathtakingly beautiful. Feel their spirit the moment you close the pages around the letter you leave. In that moment, you are connected.

beyond // Everyone, everywhere, deserves to dive into new worlds, worlds that we have loved and found home inside, and books provide an amazing way to do that, to escape, if for a moment. Donate a copy of your favorite book or books to a local women's or homeless shelter. Fill the inside cover with your own words, dedications, and well wishes for those who find it. Treat these books like Buddhist prayer flags, each of them designed to find its way into the world, little prayers, little wishes, little hopes. Words make amazing gifts, and some of us need them so much more than we may even realize.

There are species of trees
with seeds hidden deep,
they need fire to flee,
and only in flames
will they spread their wings
and land sweetly
in newly black soil.
Only when it all burns down
can they grow new.
They will carry the taste of ash
as long as they live,
their rings will sing
of the heat they endured,
but of all the trees
they will reach highest,
none will know the sky
like them.

break it down, build it up

Sometimes, some chaotic and terrifying and vital times, it all must burn down to begin again. Without the flames, without the fire and ash, new growth could never emerge, new life could never sprout through, throwing green like a promise onto the dark soot of all that was. We mourn the burnt trees, the forest reduced to diamond-glinting blackness holding the scattered sunlight, and we remember the sound of the wind through them when they stood, tall, proud. In this, we forget the new growth, the saplings reaching for light, the deadfall turned into fuel for life to restart. We forget the forest that will one day come again. Sometimes in these gorgeous lives of ours, we have to break it and burn it all down to build it back up. Sometimes we must set fire to the excuses we've been holding, the weights we've been carrying, and warm ourselves by the glow. We so deeply treasure broken things, things we have outgrown, that we forget we can choose where they go, when they go, and that we can start new. We get lost in the forest of broken limbs and fallen giants, we lose the sunlight, we lose ourselves. No more.

challenge // The bestselling book *The Life-Changing Magic of Tidying Up* probably said this better than I ever could, but I want you to break it all down to build it back up. Sift through your life, not just your closet, and figure out all the ways you've been holding on to elements of your past that simply no longer work. We change, we grow, we transform into new creatures all the time, but sometimes, we carry with us traits and ideals, relationships, fears, apprehensions, and worries that no longer fit the people we have become. Take a deeper look at the different things in your life that feel heavy, that feel harmful, that feel like they are holding you back from new growth, be it in your creative pursuits, or your endeavors to be a better, more well-rounded human being. We all have these, dozens, hundreds of them, and we bring them along from place to place, from point to point in our lives without a second thought; we assume that because we had them then, we must need them now. We rarely stop to think that perhaps closing some doors will lead to the triumphant opening of others. Now is the time to check all our open doors and figure out which ones could safely, and gently, be closed. None of these closures have to be permanent; the wonderful thing about doors is that they open both ways, and I'm not suggesting you lock them, that you actually burn them down, but rather consider keeping them shut for a time.

beyond // Even freshly burned forests need sunlight and fresh water to grow back again. So too do we. Once you've figured out all the different things you no longer have to carry, all the weights you can finally set down, look forward, and look at what you need to fulfill those creative pursuits, those endeavors, into being that better, more well-rounded person. What are you missing? Make a list of what you need to advance, to grow into something more, something you've been aiming toward. Dive into the truth of what you may be lacking, from a base level all the way up to the extras you may tell yourself are luxuries, and write next to them what you'd need to do to have them, to be them. This is self-truth time, and all I'm asking is for you to be honest with yourself on what you need to do, see, think, and find to reach the goals you have for yourself.

A million birds move above me,
I could not paint this.
They make a sound of their own,
the individual songs combining
to something new,
something louder, and I hear it
still.
Take away everything else,
and it's moments like these
that remain. I will see this
before my eyes shut
for the final time.

slow down

I live in a big state, the fourth largest in the United States, and we Montanans do not measure distance in miles, we measure them in hours. In short, there are no shortcuts. Over the course of a lifetime spent wandering into and out of Montana, this reality has planted a seed I never expected to take root, much less blossom. In me, there is a deep understanding that when presented with options on how to get from one point to another, we have a choice between the shortcut and the scenic route. Clearly, living in a state where everything is a scenic route, I am biased, and this choice never has felt much like one at all, but alas, there is a lesson in this.

We are a society that has created superhighways when we already had back roads, fiber-optic options when dial-up still connected us to the internet. We are a society that creates supercars that can break speed records, airplanes that can cross the Atlantic Ocean in three hours, fighter jets that push the envelope of technological and human endurance beyond what we perceived as the breaking point. We create shortcuts. It's what we do, it's what we've always done. Somewhere in all this speed, we lose ourselves and we lose that age-old cliché that it's not about the destination, but the journey to get there. We lose this and we never look back, in the name of progress, of efficiency, of that altogether terrifying cult of busyness. We find ourselves at these destinations we thought so vital with little or no knowledge of how we actually came to be where we ended up. Why?

challenge //

We have always had the power to slow things down. I know how easy it is to believe with fierce conviction that because everyone else is busy, we must always be as well. That we have to keep pace with the rate society presents us with, that we cannot fall behind, even for a moment. We have that power, and I'm going to try to help you remind yourself. Try this on for size: As many times as humanly possible, take the scenic route. Take the slow road, the blue highways, the road less traveled, as Robert Frost so eloquently wrote. Take the bike instead of the car, your feet instead of a cab, and allow yourself to wander. Take time in all the things you do, being mindful of every detail of whatever it is you're doing. The journey IS the destination, and it's only when we allow ourselves to stop worrying about how quickly we can accomplish the things on our to-do list, how quickly we can arrive, and sink into each adventure, each task, as if it's the only thing that matters. There is a Buddhist koan that many call the "wash your bowl" koan, and it's something I revisit mentally often. It says this:

A monk said to Chao Chou, "I have just entered this monastery.
    Please teach me."
Chao Chou said, "Have you eaten your rice gruel?"
The monk said, "Yes, I have."
Chao Chou said, "Wash your bowl."
The monk understood.

Interpret this as you will, but for me, it all circles back to mindfulness, and it all circles back to choosing to do everything with purpose instead of as a step toward the next thing to be done. If we spend our lives taking shortcuts to get to the next thing on our list, the next city on our itinerary, the next weekend, date, holiday, or experience, we are missing the point of all this. We are losing so many memories, revelations, understandings, and connections by constantly trying to arrive somewhere, constantly trying to bypass the journey in favor of the destination. Of my poetry, I am asked on a daily basis how I never run out of things to write about after all these years of posting every day. This is always my answer: If you open your eyes, if you truly see, we are surrounded by inspiration, we are surrounded by more miracles than we could ever have enough words for. We are surrounded, if only we choose to slow down, and allow it all to come into focus. Start. Now.

beyond // Make the mundane feel miraculous, and shine a light on it, illuminate it in a way it's never been illuminated before. It is easy to slow down, to appreciate, to study and get lost in beautiful things like road trips, adventures, or wandering walks. What's harder, monumentally so, is finding the miraculous in the absolutely mundane. Let's face it, we all have tasks we're presented with on a daily basis that are, for lack of a better term, boring. They are the routine but necessary things we have to do, over and over again, to make our lives run how they should run. This time around, we're going miracle hunting in the midst of all that drudgery. Take on the tasks you are often irritated by, and do them slowly, with intent and care, searching for the details that you may have lost in the process. Hate doing the dishes? Do them this time with your focus on the smell of the soap, the temperature of the water, the rhythm of your hands washing, then drying. The satisfaction of making dirty things clean. Hate taking out the garbage? Look for birds, listen for their songs, smell the air, feel the wind, see how far you can hear, the layers and layers of sound; when you find your way back inside, write about all you saw, all you felt, smelled, experienced. Sometimes the slow road reveals itself in strange and beautiful ways— it's our job to recognize them.

Find the quirks
that fill in the spaces
between the letters
in your name,
find them and highlight
them, shout
them out.
I wish you knew how
little
it mattered
what anyone, anywhere
thinks of them.
You are perfect
only because
you are different.

a self-portrait

From selfie sticks to mobile phones, FaceTime to facial-recognition software in social media accounts spread across the internet, we're bombarded with images of ourselves these days. We're presented with dozens of opportunities each day to see ourselves, the features that make us unique, that make us who we are, but still, we don't really seem to see ourselves. We are so often blind to the beauty, we forget to stop and appreciate what we are seeing. We compare ourselves, unnaturally but constantly, to the false ideal we're inundated with. Next to those perfect people, we tell ourselves, we must be plain, we must be ordinary. So quickly does our attention shift to any of the hundreds of distractions our lives present us, that we push ourselves aside, and before we understand how it happens, we're completely unaware of just how unique we truly are. How completely unordinary we've always been.

challenge //

I'm going to be totally up-front here—
I am probably the world's worst when it comes to drawing, and so I'm
not going to pretend that there's only one way of accomplishing this
challenge. I am a writer and I am a photographer, I always have been,
and so when I complete this challenge, my ink will be words, and it will
be with a photograph, but I urge you to choose whatever medium feels
most natural or sincere to you. I would like you to create a self-portrait.
I do not care which artistic medium you choose, once again, but I want
you to create a piece that is you, that highlights the features, both phys-
ical and otherwise, that constitute you, that make you the exquisite mir-
acle you've always been. You can use ink, you can use words, you can
use cameras and film, you can use clay, you can use a coded computer
program or website, as long as you create a piece of art that is you,
in all your glory. Take your time, look into the photographs you are in,
look into mirrors, look into yourself, and give yourself the attention and
appreciation you deserve. Think of this as a caricature in reverse. In-
stead of comically highlighting the features that may stand out (for me,
that's my big nose or ears), you're going to highlight the features you
find beautiful. You're going to draw or paint, photograph or poetically
describe, the magic that is you.

beyond // We all know where we come from, though we may forget from time to time. We know what we've been through that has led us here, to this place, to this person. We just spent time creating a portrait of ourselves, an honest look at the people we are, the beauty we have but forget to notice, the extraordinary people we don't like admitting we are. We know this, but who will we be? Who do we wish to be? Five, ten, twenty, or fifty years from this day, what will we look like, what will we be proud of, what will we mourn, regret, and appreciate? What features would we paint then, be it with words or photography, ink or clay? Now is your chance to find out. I want you to create a second self-portrait, not of who you are now, but of who you will be, who you *want* to be then. Fill this portrait with the same amount of care, of attention to detail, of sincerity. Who will you be, years from this day? Show yourself, then show us.

It's about finding your passions
and giving them the respect
they deserve.
It's about recognizing that
low days will come, understanding
that they are not who you are,
and certainly not who you will become,
but what you are going through.
Nothing more.
Some days I fade like smoke from myself,
all that remains is the scent
of where the rest of me stood;
other days I'm flame fire without a trace
of rising ash.
Neither is wrong, neither
is more.

"The Great Adventure . . .

passion over perceived perfection

It's a natural thing, looking at images of people's lives we perceive as perfect and wishing we had what they had. We are assaulted on a daily basis by curated lives in curated squares, social media showing us snippets of seemingly perfect lives. We are lied to, and we build up our own expectations all around this foundation of untruth. We aim our sights not at our passions, but at this perfection we think we should have. We expect someone else's passions to mold themselves around us, to become ours. Inevitably, we become monumentally distraught when this doesn't work out, when it doesn't fit, doesn't custom-form around the way our minds work, how our inherent natures tend to flow. Somewhere along the way, we stopped paying attention to what makes our own hearts race and started focusing on the joy and passion that others have found. We see theirs and we want it for ourselves, but we forget that first step: finding our passions, and understanding that they only work once we do find them, if we work with them, for them.

challenge //

Grab a sheet of paper and your favorite writing utensil and give yourself some time to truly reflect. Make a list of the moments in your life you have felt the most alive, the most centered, the most passionate, and, truly, the most like the *you* you've always wanted to be. Describe in as much detail as you can where you were, what you were doing, how it made you feel, and why. Make this list long and make it honest. When you've exhausted yourself of these fond and passionate memories, go back through and read everything you've written. Make note of the parts that stand out the most in your own memory, the pieces that seem to highlight themselves cinematically when you recall them. These are the seeds of passion that you cannot fake, these are the unwatered little pieces that, if given time and space and attention and respect, can one day blossom, can one day bloom. What are the threads that tie them together? What does your passion look like, not your perfection? Finding our own passions is the absolute cornerstone of living a more joyful, mindful, and wonderful life. We get so wrapped up in chasing perfection, we forget to define it for ourselves. We forget to seek. When we find this, when we discover that common thread that connects all the most connected and happy moments of our lives, we can make another list, a list that describes all we must do to make that passion work for us. Develop your passion actively, daily, constantly. Do not think that passion will magically do it for you. Understanding that it is growth, more than it is a static dive into passionate waters, that will push us into who we wish to be. We can learn what we must do to take what wakes up our souls, and make it our realities.

beyond // The name of this game is research. We are surrounded by curated museums of perceived perfection, of people "living their best life," and we begin to convince ourselves we need it too. Now is your chance to chase not after their perfection, but rather the underlying passion that drives them to it. Contact five people you follow on social media, pay attention to, or admire, and ask not how they wandered into their "perfect" lives, but how they figured out what their passion was. How did they begin doing what they are doing, before it became the profitable and enviable pursuit it may have become? Asking people you respect and admire how they came to be where they ended up can often show us not only stark differences but startling similarities. Sometimes we are standing in front of doors we locked ourselves, holding the key but still calling the locksmith. Listen, learn, and apply the knowledge to your own pursuit of passion.

If you wait for beauty to
present itself,
it may, a time or two,
half dozen or so
over the winding course
of your life. If you
choose to find it on your own,
your eyes
will never have time
to close.

be creative
every day

Of all the bits and baubles of this book, this penultimate one, I hope, stays with you. I hope it burns, engraves, embroiders, tattoos, photographs, paints, types, sketches, knits, dances, sings, plays, composes, acts, sculpts, builds, designs, sews, and doodles itself permanently into your heart and mind. I hope wherever you go from here, from these final pages, you take this one with you and you let it grow and spread and take over your life like vines, like a field of wildflowers after a long-awaited rain. I don't know what you got out of this book. It was, and is, an experiment on sharing things I've learned along the way here, of passing on any information, however valuable or invaluable, and hoping you find even a single sentence that helps you find pieces of yourself you gave up on as lost. I don't know if you got two pages in and skipped to the end, I don't know if you treasured every challenge, and I won't know unless you tell me, but I will hope. So before I leave you to wander through these final pages, before I shut my mouth and let you do what you will with this book, share it or hide it away, toss it or treasure it, I'll leave you with one final thought, a thought that quite honestly carries me through every single day of my life and makes me feel more like myself than maybe any other. It is this: Be creative every single day. Even if it is once, even if you have to force it for a long, long while before it comes naturally, even if you have to invent new ways to find it, be creative. Make it a purposeful thing, make it intentional, make it habitual, and make it a priority. We live busy lives, all of us inundated and surrounded by a million things to steal our attention and time. I know the threat is real and abundant, and I know how easy it is to excuse away missing a day here or there. I also know how simple it is for one day to turn into five, five days into five months, months into years. Too many of us let our creativity, and therefore our passions, fall away and vanish, dusted over by years of busyness and priority. No more. Creativity is at the heart of all this, and creation is the key. It is so easy to tear down, to pick apart and point out flaws. It is so easy to destroy. Creation, creativity, is hard.

challenge // This one is going to take a while, and this one is going to be all up to you. The challenge itself is simple, but it's the toughest one in this book to stick with. *Do something creative every single day.* At least one something, preferably dozens, hundreds. I do not care if you paint, write, draw, type, dance, sing, build, sculpt, or any of the other artistic and creative pursuits this world has to offer; I do not care if your creativity leaks out in the form of compassion aimed at those who may not deserve it, in self-guided meditation; I do not care if you make a snowman, sand castle, or paper airplane. There are no rules to any of this, other than finding, no, *making* the time to be creative at least once a day. I believe creativity unlocks so much more in our lives, from compassion to much-needed relief from anxiety or depression. I believe creativity is a fire that spreads all through our lives, painting everything in its ash and allowing new growth to emerge. I believe creativity is the key to joy, as it's the key to curiosity, to that desire to understand more, and to help others understand us more. Creativity is the thing, it's the spark that starts us on fire, and we can guarantee that flame stays burning. Once a day, or more if you can, do something creative. It can take moments or it can take hours, it can be one project that spans months or it can be a month of projects spanning a day each, it doesn't matter. Be creative, every day, and watch what happens. Watch how your eyes change, watch how the world changes, watch how you change.

beyond //

This is optional, as I know not everyone is as certifiably insane as I am, but as I honestly attribute every accomplishment in my life and career to this beyond challenge, I'm going to give it to you, and I'm going to leave it there. Almost a decade ago, I challenged myself to write a daily haiku on love, literally every single day. No skipping days. No forgetting. No excuses. Almost ten years later, I have never missed a single day. It changed my life. It forced me, every morning, to find myself in a creative mind-set, to think outside the box, to create. A few years in, it was this daily ritual that started the other daily ritual that would lead me here, lead me to all of you. I started my Typewriter Series following the same guideline, forcing myself every day to write a poem, no excuses. As I began working on this new book, I am at over six years without ever slipping. Six years of poetry, of pouring my heart out into words, and as I revisit them now, they feel like journal entries, they feel like a diary I never intended on creating. It opened my life up and gave me strange and wonderful opportunities I never saw coming. It can for you too. Set a daily challenge for yourself in the creative pursuit you most enjoy. If it's writing, challenge yourself to write a poem, a haiku, even a single sentence; if it's photography you love, take a photo, even if it's just one, every single day. Whatever your art, find a small way to practice it once a day, always. No exceptions. Do this until the passion for it fades, and then begin something new. Hold yourself to this, force it, and create a ritual out of it. You never know where you could end up.

Wasted life living
for some day,
some far off
time, when it all lines
up. Wasted
in the wishing and waiting
and the slow decay
of the perfection
that is now.
Go. Seek.
Find and discover.
Home is where you
fall in love
with yourself.

seek,
simply seek

Is there a more isolating trait than complacency? Few things have the ability to remove us from the splendor that surrounds us than complete complacency in the face of it. We fall into lethargy from time to time, convincing ourselves that when it comes to all we are enveloped in, we've seen it all, done it all, and experienced it all before. We lie to ourselves and fall into the altogether apathetic view that there is nothing new to behold, nothing exciting left to discover. How many marvels are we overlooking in this laze? How many life-changing, mind-blowing, perspective-altering things are we leaving behind as we wallow in the mistaken belief that it's not worth it to explore? What is the consequence of this, what pieces of ourselves are we sacrificing as we risk nothing and stay safely in the comfort of the world we have created? When it comes to pure inspiration, quite simply, we are risking everything, each piece of ourselves that so desperately needs it. When we stop seeking, we stop finding. And when we stop finding, we stop growing.

challenge //

On the surface of all things, this is probably the simplest-looking challenge in this little book. To seek, simply seek, sounds deceptively easy, like a no-brainer tidbit that makes you roll your eyes and think it is a waste of breath, of ink, of time. I think you'll be surprised, perhaps pleasantly, perhaps you'll be slightly irritated with me at how challenging it can be to actually seek, but whatever the case, I'm betting it's not the simple task you might believe. Go and seek beauty, hidden pieces of it, pieces you can capture with photographs, with brief descriptions on notebooks in your pocket, or with the perfect haze of your own memory. Seek hidden gems on popular streets, seek back alleys with stories of their own. Seek long drives with windows down, seek train conversations as the world rushes by outside. Seek joyful encounters, seek meaningful interactions, seek delicious tastes from unknown foods, seek music that shuts your eyes and spreads goose bumps like wildflower seeds on your skin. Wake each day with truly seeking on your mind, and make it a priority, not an option. Open your eyes and seek out light streaming through tree leaves, through buildings, off windows, onto puddles at your feet. Seek stillness amidst the sound, amidst the noise of it all, seek compassion in the face of hatred, in the face of animosity and unkindness. Seek life, all things that breathe, that grow, that seek out the sunlight for themselves, seek the dark and twisted paths and wave at those on the straight and narrow. Seek those who need our love, our kindness, our tender grace, and give it to them without a single thought of seeking it returned. Seek laughter, belly-aching, body-shaking, mind-tickling laughter that leaves you breathless and awake; seek the stunning shine of your own sorrow, and your ability to overcome it. Seek understanding when you sink low, when you feel the weight of all things slowly crushing you, and seek the knowledge that you can rise above it, always, and have before. Above all things, seek passion, for every moment you're alive. Seek the heart-pulsing reminder that we get to choose how we look at the days we're given, the hours we receive like a gift each day, the minutes we can fill with as much passion as we wish. Seek to spread it, everywhere, and make yours infectious to everyone who wanders into your life. Seek passion, and watch others seek theirs. So much beauty lives right beyond your inability to go looking; stop waiting for it to show up on your doorstep, and go invite it in. Seek. Just seek, and never, ever, stop.

acknowledgments

//

I am a man made of many, a combination of those I love, and those who love me back. I am composed of all who have helped me, all who encouraged, taught, supported, and believed, but also all those who didn't. Thank you feels too small sometimes, and in this case, abundantly so. Nevertheless, I need to say it.

First, and always foremost, thank you to Sarah Linden, my best friend, my fellow Chaser of the Light, my silly heart beating outside of my chest, for helping me find my feet, and believing they were born with wanderlust in them. Thank you for creating this book with me, but more, for loving me and creating a life I am so proud to live. I'll never stop trying to repay you, though I'll never succeed.

Thank you to my parents, Jan and Goose Gregson, who taught me what love is, what it can endure, and for embracing my oddities with open arms.

Thank you to my sisters, McGraw Donovan and Rian Oliver, for being my best friends, my magical nomadic childhood wanderers, the most wonderful people and mothers I have ever known, and for making me an uncle four times over.

Thank you to my agent, Rachel Vogel, for knowing exactly what's best for me, and constantly fighting for it. For understanding this strange brain of mine, and honestly, for making all of this happen, and always believing it would.

Thank you to Lauren Appleton, Marian Lizzi, Meg Leder, John Duff, Farin Schlussel, Casey Maloney, Lindsay Gordon, and everyone else behind the scenes at Penguin Random House and TarcherPerigee. You took a chance on me, and I am forever in your debt for doing so. I will never stop trying to prove your risk is one worth taking.

Thank you to the first-ever class of Chasers of the Light, all you brave souls who bared yours and signed up for a crazy online course on a whim and mission to change your lives for the better. Thank you for trusting us to help show you that way.

Thank you to all of you, the readers, the fans, the friends I haven't yet met, for caring enough about the rain in this brain to support me over these years. I wouldn't be here without you.

Finally, thank you to Henry and Adela, for letting me try my best at raising you, at making you into rad little humans, even though I'm learning as I go. Thank you to Patrick Donovan; Wes Oliver; my nieces and nephews: Griffin, Winslow, Banks, and Moyer; Calvin and Hobbes; A.K.; Meannie; NarNar and Papa; Brianna Yamashita; Jenna Block; Oleg Lyubner; Howie Sanders; Jason Richman; Christina Perri; Greg Dorrington; Gregory Alan Isakov; Edgar and Jenny; Pete and Lisa; Deb and Mike; and for everyone else for every role you played, none were too small.

about the author

//

Tyler Knott Gregson is a poet, photographer, artist, and author. If he's not writing, he's making photographs all over the world with his partner in crime, Sarah Linden, as part of Chasers of the Light, Inc.

Find him at chasersofthelight.com and @tylerknott on all of the social media things you can probably think of.

//

also by tyler knott gregson

//